Designing Computer Programs

Designing Computer Programs

Jim Haigh

formerly Peterborough Regional College

Edward Arnold
A member of the Hodder Headline Group
LONDON   MELBOURNE   AUCKLAND

First published in Great Britain in 1995 by
Edward Arnold, a division of Hodder Headline PLC,
338 Euston Road, London NW1 3BH

British Library Cataloguing in Publication Data
A catalogue record for this book is available from the British Library

ISBN 0 340 61398 X

1 2 3 4 5   95 96 97 98 99

Typeset in Palatino by GreenGate Publishing Services, Tonbridge, Kent
Printed and bound in Great Britain by the Bath Press, Avon

Contents

Preface

The aim of the book

The aim of the book is to provide a simple introduction to structured program design for complete beginners. As far as is known, at the time of writing, there is no other such book on the market.

All syllabuses that include an element of programming, such as

- Intermediate GNVQ in Information Technology: Optional and/or Additional units
- Advanced GNVQ in Information Technology: Optional and/or Additional units
- the BTEC National Diploma in Computer Studies
- the Foundation Diploma of the IDPM
- the 'Coding and Programming' modules of the City & Guilds 7261 in Basic, Pascal, 'C' and Cobol
- the GCSEs in Computer Studies
- the 'A' levels in Computer Science

require the student to make at least a beginning in program design, and it is the author's experience that this should be introduced right at the start. Once a student has become used to writing programs without first producing a design, even if it is a rough one, it is hard to break the habit. It is much easier to start as one means to go on.

The book should be suitable for school pupils, for 65 year olds having a go at programming in retirement, and for anyone else in between who has never designed a program before. Those who have done some flowcharting may have some trouble at first, adjusting to the structured approach, but a little perseverance will overcome the problem.

The book and the designs are not language specific and they should be suitable for any block-structured procedural language such as the more modern Basics, Cobol, Pascal and C. The author did not have in mind programs written for machine tools or games.

Some courses require students to have some appreciation of program design, without expecting them to learn a language or do any coding. The book should provide a valuable introduction.

The book has deliberately been made short, both to make it affordable and to encourage anyone who fears that to learn the fundamentals of program design will be long and difficult. In consequence, it does not cover fully syllabuses such as City & Guilds 7261-238 'Elementary Program Design Techniques'.

Need

Most books on programming claim to include program design. The treatment is often very brief, and it is seldom carried through. Some authors skip the subject altogether, claiming that it is dealt with in other books. All existing books on program design as a separate topic are unsuitable for beginners, with the possible exception of degree students. Yet program design is essential if programming is not simply to become hacking. It has rightly been said that any fool can write programs, but to write good programs needs real skill.

Approach

The means of expressing designs will be the structure diagram, with accompanying action lists and condition lists. The diagrams will be compatible with JSP (Jackson Structured Programming), but Jackson's rigorous approach, from data structures, will not be used, as it is too difficult for beginners. The reasons for this choice are:

- Students are, in the author's experience, much more willing to draw diagrams than write pseudocode. It is essential to have a method that students will actually use. It is no use if they give up, and write code first and then do the 'design' afterwards.
- Flowcharts are snares that lead directly to unstructured code. As Michael Jackson says in his book *The Principles of Program Design*, 'Flowcharting is not designing. Design is about structure, and flowcharts, as their name suggests, are about flow of control. . So we will draw no more flowcharts'.
- JSP is widely taught on degree and other GNVQ level 4 courses. The method used in this book should be a good stepping stone to that.

Program design language (PDL), sometimes called pseudocode, will be introduced and used in Chapter 9.

How to use the book

The book could be read in its entirety before any coding was attempted; it could be used along with a course on a particular programming language, and so be accompanied by coding at every stage; or coding could be started, independently, once the reader was about half way through the book, so that the two were overlapped. The second of these possibilities might present problems, because the simplest designs are not always implemented by the simplest parts of a programming language.

The book could also be used by someone who had unfortunately learned to code without learning anything about design, and had come to see – perhaps the hard way – that design is useful and important.

Apart from Chapter 1, which can be read at any point, the book is intended to be read in sequence. Reading however, is only part of the story. The student is urged to study the example designs carefully and thoroughly, and to do the exercises at the ends of the chapters. Answers are provided, so that the reader can check on his or her work. It is important to note that there is often more than one right answer to even very simple programming problems, so those given are not the only possible ones.

The book should lend itself best to resource based learning, now being used more and more in further education colleges. But it should also be fine for self study, and for class use. It would be valuable if the student could have his or her answers looked at by a tutor because, as just mentioned, a solution might be right even though it is different from the one at the back. Conversely, what might appear to the student to be only a slight error might be very important.

Jim Haigh
Peterborough, 1994

Glossary

(Note: the definitions given here are only basic definitions, adequate for the understanding of this book.)

*. The symbol * has two meanings in this book. If it is in the top right corner of a box it is the symbol for repetition. It means the box may be repeated. It is also the symbol for multiplication. 3 * 4 = 12. In this case it is an example of an arithmetic operator.

Abnormal termination. The formal term for 'crash'. It describes the stopping of a program before it should because something has gone wrong. A perfectly correct program would never terminate abnormally (unless it were used in a way that was never intended when it was specified).

Cell. A place in main memory where an item of data can be stored. Data has to be in main memory before it can be worked on. See also: *Variable*.

Controlling variable. A variable used in a program to count the passes through a repetition and to cause it to repeat the desired number of times. See *For*.

Data name. See *Variable*.

Data type. A class of variable (see below). When a variable is declared (created) it has to be given both a name and a type. Its type will govern what the program can do with the contents. Types are of some importance at the design stage, for three reasons:
1. There are usually restrictions on transferring data from a variable of one type to a variable of another.
2. Only if a variable is of numeric type will the program be able to do arithmetic with the contents.
3. If the type is numeric but the contents are not (a situation that can easily exist with raw input data), and arithmetic is attempted, the program will crash.

Decrement. To make smaller, usually by one. To subtract 1 from.

Execute. When the instructions contained in a program are being carried out by the computer, we say that the computer is executing the program. A program written by you will have to be converted into machine code (compiled) before it can be executed.

Eof. End of file. This may be a flag or a function that can be tested to see if the end of the file has been reached.

Flag. A variable used to show the state of something in a program. For example a flag may show, after checking, whether the input data was valid or not.

For. A kind of repetition in which there is a variable, called the controlling variable, that is incremented or decremented automatically at the end of each repeat.

Identifier. Another name for *Variable*.

Increment. To make larger, usually by one. To add 1 to.

Initialize. To give a value to a variable either at the beginning of a program or just before the start of a repeat. If totalling is going to be done, the variable to be used must be initialized to zero. Numeric variables are usually initialized to 0 or 1. E.g. Let grand_total = 0. Non-numeric variables are often initialized to spaces.

Integer. A whole number. It may be negative or positive. Examples: 2, 3456, − 17, 0, − 1, 1000000.

Iterate. To carry out zero, one or many times. Means the same as *Repeat*.

Literal. A literal is a number or word that appears in the program and is used or output exactly as it stands. Non-numeric literals go in quotes. Some programming languages use double quotes (") and others use single quotes ('). An example of a numeric literal is 98.4. An example of a non-numeric literal is 'C 778 XLA'.

Location. A location in main memory. Means the same as *Cell*.

Numeric. Capable of arithmetic. This may refer to data or it may refer to a data type. See data type above.

Procedure. A kind of subprogram or subroutine. In this book, a box with a name in it is potentially a procedure.

Refinement. When a program is more than very small, the first structure diagram drawn will be an overview which does not show all the details. That is, some of the boxes will not have actions below them. The detail of such boxes is decided later. The process of gradually going into more and more detail is called refinement.

Repeat. To carry out zero, one or many times. Means the same as Iterate.

String. A variable type. A variable is usually declared as string when it is expected that the contents might be anything. (The data in it are 'strung' together.) A string variable is not suitable for arithmetic.

Subroutine. A portion of a program that has in some way been separated off, so that it can be designed separately or coded separately or tested separately. A subroutine can usually be entered or called from anywhere in the main program.

Subscript. A number or a numeric variable that is being used to point to a particular element in an array.

Test after. see *Test before*.

Test before. All repetitions must be brought to an end at some point. A condition is tested to see whether the program should enter the repeated code or move on to the next part of the program. If the condition is tested before entering the repeated code each time this is 'test before'. If the condition is tested each time the end of the repeated code is reached this is 'test after'. With test after the code to be repeated is always executed at least once. With test before it may be repeated zero times.

Variable. A variable is the name of a cell in main memory, and also the name of the data in it. The variable name is invented by the programmer. It is a great help if the name indicates clearly what the cell is to be used for. Examples of names that might be used are: page_number, quantity_in_stock, and date_of_birth. Other words in common use that mean almost exactly the same as variable are: **identifier**, **data-name**, and **field**. All programming languages have **Reserved words** that cannot be used as variable names. If such a word is used in a design it will have to be changed slightly before coding. In Pascal, C and Cobol the programmer has to name (or **declare**) the variables before using them, as is done in this book in the variable lists. In Basic this is not necessary.

Variable list. A list of the variables that will be needed in the program. All the variables listed should appear in the Action list or the Condition list or both.

Variable names in the text

In this book, any word in the text that is in italics and starts with a capital letter is a variable name. It should appear in a variable list nearby. Variable names in the action, condition and variable lists do not have capital letters.

Bold type is used for emphasis. All words in the index are printed in bold in the text the first time they are used. (Not all words in bold are in the index, though.)

There are answers at the back of the book to all exercises, except those marked with an asterisk (*).

The steps in program design

1. Compose a *small* amount of input data.
2. Work out, and write down, the expected outcomes.
3. Make a note of the steps taken in working out the results. The purpose of these first three steps is to make sure that you fully understand the nature of the input and output data, and the processing necessary to get from one to the other.
4. Make lists of variables as far as possible.
5. Write down, maybe informally, the main repetitions and their controlling conditions.*
6. Write down, maybe informally, the main activities.*
7. Formalize the conditions.*
8. Write an action list.*
9. Draw a first attempt at a diagram.
10. Allocate the actions and conditions to the diagram.
11. Improve the diagram.
12. Dry run the design.
13. Alter the three lists and the diagram as necessary.
14. Repeat steps 12 and 13 until the design is satisfactory.

* Add to the variable lists as necessary.

1

Introduction

The method used in the book does not claim to remove the need for inspiration entirely, but it does claim to reduce it considerably. The method helps the student develop a design in several ways. It removes the problem of knowing where to begin, by setting out a series of steps which can be followed for almost any programming problem at the introductory level. It breaks the problem down into manageable pieces. It encourages the continual setting down of ideas, facts and logic on paper. This helps to avoid the two great enemies: muddle and confusion. Where inspiration is needed, this is greatly aided by the facts and names available on paper, and the understanding of the problem that has been gained at earlier stages.

By the end of the book you should be able to tackle confidently the sort of problem that follows. A full design will be found in Chapter 10.

The program simulates a supermarket checkout.

Inputs

1. At start of day, a stock-and-prices file is read into a table in main store. This file has, for each kind of good, many fields, but the only ones read into main store are:
   - stock number (4 digits + check digit)
   - description (15 characters)
   - price (in pence, max 9999)
   - quantity in stock (an integer, max 5000)

   Also obtained, via the operating system or the keyboard, is the date.
2. As each checkout clerk comes on duty, she keys in an identification number (an id). These are preceded by the letter I.
3. At end of day, the letter E is keyed. Confirmation is asked for, and given by the letter Y.
4. For each item purchased, a stock number. This actually comes from a bar-code scanner, but you can simulate it by keying in a 5

digit 'self-checking' number.
5. For each customer, a method of payment and an amount tendered, preceded by the number 2, keyed instead of a stock number. The date and the time will also be used. If possible, both should come from the operating system, but if your programming language does not have the facilities for accessing them, they may be simulated as follows: the date is keyed in at the beginning of the day, when the program is first loaded. Time is not used. Instead, each customer is given a serial number, starting from one when each clerk comes on duty.

Method of payment will be C for cash, Q for cheque, R for credit card, or D for debit card. Amount tendered will be in pence.

Outputs

For each customer, printed on paper, a receipt showing

the shop name, Freshfare

the name and price of each item purchased

a total amount due

an item count

the amount tendered

the change due

the date, the clerk's id, and either the time or a serial no.

On screen, the price, as each item is 'scanned'. As soon as a customer's bill is totalled, the amount due replaces this on the screen.

In main memory (not a real output, but a simulated one), an update to the quantity in stock for each item from the stock file, in main store.

On disk

(a) a total of the value of sales, and number of items for each operative, for her stint or shift.
(b) a total of the value of sales, and number of items for the day, before the program is terminated, on close of business.

The prices file, written back at the end of the day, with the updated quantities on it.

Processing

Most of the processing needed is obvious from the descriptions of the input and output. The check digit on the stock number is calculated as follows. The digits are weighted, the check digit itself having a weight of one, and the leftmost digit a weight of 5.

Each digit is multiplied by its weighting, and the resulting products are added. The resulting total is divided by 11. The remainder should be zero. If it is not, the number is invalid. The cashier can then try again. (Numbers that would require a check digit of 10 are not used.)

Language independence

The method used for the designs is language independent. The author has had in mind Pascal, C, Cobol-85 and modern versions of Basic. The translation of a very simple design into code, for all four of these languages, is demonstrated in Chapter 4.

Limitations

No attempt is made anywhere to include instructions that merely enhance the appearance of output. For example, all references to clearing the screen, and such niceties as the positioning of a message at a particular spot on a screen, are omitted. They have little if anything to do with design in the sense in which it is used in this text, which is really about logic. They are much more to do with the programming language that will be used.

Why bother with design?

Why not? A program is a complicated product like a car, an office block, or a microwave oven. Would any company try to produce such things without first drawing up careful and detailed designs? Of course not. If they did, the things they made would be of such poor quality that they would fail to sell and the company would very soon go out of business.

Students are often misled because the first programs that they write are very small, far smaller than any useful commercial program. Such small programs may not need designing, in the way that a small, crude hut may not need designing. Later, when the programs reach a size that makes design important, the student may not know how to go about design or may have developed bad habits, or both. It is much better to start as you mean to go on, and draw designs right from the word go. That way the design techniques are learnt when the programs are small and simple. Trying to do your first designs when the programs have become large or complicated really is difficult. Having to bother with design may seem a chore, but struggling with a program that never seems to work properly whatever you do is frustrating and unpleasant.

Programs ought to be as easy as possible to maintain, and robust. Most programs need bringing up to date from time to time. Most programs need improving to make them more useful to the user. Most commercial-sized programs contain errors, and these need correcting. For all these reasons, programs have to be modified. They should therefore be written in such a way that changes can be made (a) easily, because that means cheaply, and (b) without upsetting them so that they no longer work properly in some respect.

The cost of correcting an error late on in the development process has been shown to be very much higher than correcting one early on. The cost of correction once the program is operational is higher still. Good program design reduces errors at the most cost-effective stage.

Large programs are often worked on by several programmers. Without design this is not possible.

Program design takes time, of course, but in general, that time is more than recovered during the lifetime of the program. If you have a deadline to meet, whether it is laid down by your boss or the examining board, getting straight into the coding might be satisfying at first. But it is usually a first-rate example of 'more haste, less speed'. Highly paid programming managers are convinced that those who design best will finish first, when program reliability and maintainablity are taken into account.

2

Structure diagrams

Computers are like ladies in tight skirts, spiders and mice: they get where they want to go using small rapid steps. One of the programmer's jobs is to devise solutions to problems that involve only small steps. Such a solution is called an **algorithm**. The structure diagram is a way of getting an algorithm down on paper, so that we can think about it, check it to see if it really works, and then code from it.

Computers do things in rather strange ways. We shall start learning a design method by looking at non-computer problems so that we don't have to deal with too many new things at once.

Sequence

We can start with a recipe – making a pot of tea. Here it is:

1. Put water in the kettle
2. Put tea-bags in the tea pot
3. Pour the boiling water into the tea pot
4. Put the lid on the pot.

To turn that recipe into a structure diagram, all we need to do is to re-write the instructions in a series of boxes from left to right, all hanging from a line above, as shown in Fig. 2.1.

The structure formed by the four plain boxes in a row, which must be followed left to right, is a **sequence**. (The meaning of 'plain' will become clear shortly.)

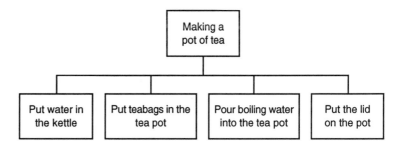

Figure 2.1

Repetition

The recipe is, though, a bit too simple. There's nothing about waiting until the water is boiling. A better diagram would be that shown in Fig. 2.2.

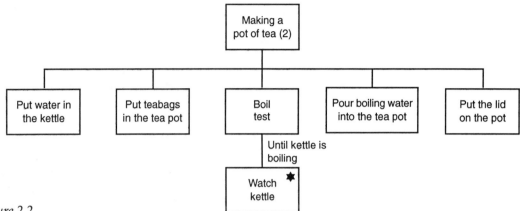

Figure 2.2

The lowest box has a star in the top right corner, and the words 'until kettle is boiling'. The star, which you will see in the next chapter is like a times sign, means that the instruction in the box is usually done many times. Confusingly, it has several names, including iteration, loop, and repetition. We shall use the word **repetition**. Although the action in the box is usually done many times, it may be done any number of times - zero times, one time, two times.... . If the kettle were boiling already, when we first glanced at it, we wouldn't watch it at all, we would go straight on to pouring.

The words following the special word UNTIL are: 'Kettle is boiling'. This is called a **condition**, and we go on repeating the action 'watch kettle' until the condition is true. The meaning of the word *condition* as used here is special and it is important to be clear about it. A condition is a short statement that is either TRUE or FALSE. It is very close to being a question to which the answer must be yes or no, such as, 'Is the the kettle boiling?' Because we can ask the yes/no question, 'Is dinner ready?', the statement, 'Dinner is ready' (which is either true or false) is a condition. Other examples of conditions would be:

It is raining
The dog is hungry
g = 6
There is more data to be processed
Quantity in stock = (3 + 8)

Relational Operators

Besides the equals sign, '=', several other symbols are used. They are called **relational operators**. They are:

>   > meaning 'is greater than'
>   < meaning 'is less than'
>   >= meaning 'is greater than or equal to'
>   <= meaning 'is less than or equal to'
>   <> meaning 'is not equal to' (In Cobol NOT = is used instead of <>, and in C ! = is used.)

A hint on remembering which is which: $2 > 1$ is TRUE. The symbol '>' starts big and gets smaller as it goes on towards the right. 2 is on the big or wide side of > and 1 is on the small or narrow side.

In the list of conditions above, in '$g = 6$', g is used as in the algebra we all do, or have done, in school. g is a variable and may stand, for example, for a mass in grams or the number of girls in a class. In computing, single letters are not often used. Instead, something fuller is used, such as mass-in-grams or girls-in-class. These would be suitable in Cobol. In other languages it might be mass_in_grams and girls_in_class or MassInGrams and GirlsInClass. In this book, all the variations will be used. When working through the exercises, the reader is advised to use names that will work in the programming language he or she is likely to be using in the near future.

Some rules

- A box with a star means repetition.
- The star is drawn in the top right corner.
- Next to the star, just outside the box, there must be a condition.
- A box with a star should be on its own, not in a row with other boxes.

Selection

The tea making algorithm is still a bit brief. What if the cook has loose tea in a packet, and no tea bags? The chart could be improved to that shown in Fig. 2.3.

The new part of the chart is two boxes with circles or 'o's in the corners and it is obvious that the cook should EITHER put tea bags in the pot, OR spoon tea into the pot, not do first one and then the other. Just above the first 'o' is a condition, 'tea in bags'. This is a condition because either the tea is in bags or it isn't. If this condition is true, the action in the left box is done, otherwise the action in the box on the

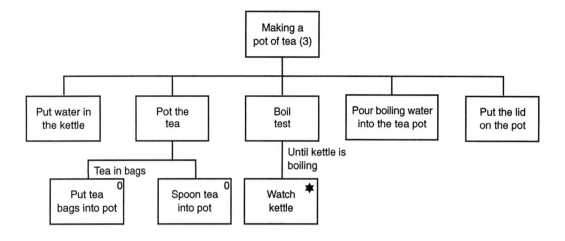

Figure 2.3

right is done. This is called a **selection**. As will be seen later, a selection may consist of more than two boxes, but for now it will be a pair, with one condition.

Some rules

- A box with an 'o' means a selection, or a choice.
- A box with an 'o' must be with another of its own kind.
- The 'o's are drawn in the top right corners.
- Boxes with 'o's should not be in a row with other kinds of boxes.
- Next to the left 'o' there must be a condition.

Sometimes, when a condition is false, nothing is to be done. For example, 'If there are dirty pots, wash up, otherwise do nothing.' This is shown by putting a short line in the right-hand box Fig. 2.4..

That's all there is to structure diagrams! The reason is that it has been proved by learned professors that any problem that can be solved by writing computer programs in languages like Basic, Pascal, Cobol and 'C', can be solved by means of an algorithm made up of only sequences, repetitions and selections. These three are called **constructs**, and no other construct is required.

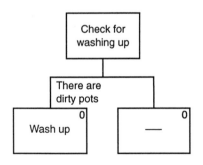

Figure 2.4

Even so, more practice will be needed because the diagram shows the solution to a problem, and problem solving needs practice. Here is another example. Mavis, who is very methodical, is about to do her Christmas cards. This is her procedure:

1. She gets out her list and brings it up-to-date.
2. She counts up how many cards she needs.
3. She buys the correct number.
4. She then prepares the cards, which means, for each one, writing in the card, writing the envelope, and then putting

the card in the envelope.

5. After preparing them all, she sorts the cards into two piles, those she is going to deliver by hand, and those she is going to post.

6. She puts stamps on the ones for the post, and takes them to the post box.

7. Finally, she delivers the others.

Condition list

C1 Until all cards done

C2 too inconvenient to deliver by hand

The conditions 'Until all cards done' and 'too inconvenient to deliver by hand' were too long to fit on the diagram in the correct place, so the numbers C1 and C2 have been used, and their meanings given in a list. Numbering the conditions and putting them in a list will be done more as we go along.

Whenever you have completed a diagram, you should check it to see if it works. This will be easier to do when we tackle computer-type questions. The checking process is called **dry running**. It will be dealt with fully in Chapter 4. At this stage, you can use your common sense to go through a diagram. The boxes in the Christmas card diagram have been given letters. This is just so that a reminder can be given of how the diagram works. The basic sequence of operations is: (b) Preliminaries, (c) Buy the cards, (d) Prepare the

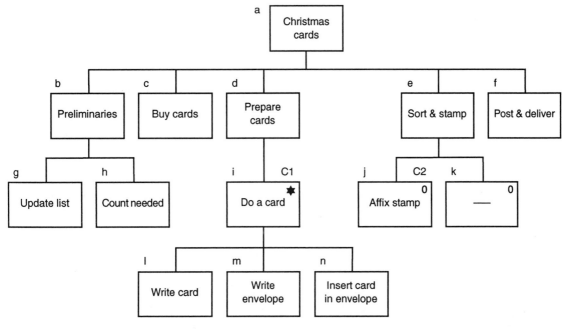

Figure 2.5

cards, (e) Sort and stamp the cards, (f) Post and deliver.

(c) and (f) are considered straightforward and no further detail is given. The meaning of 'b Preliminaries' is given as 'g Update list' and 'h Count quantity needed'. The meaning of 'd Prepare the cards' is shown as a repetition of (i) 'Do a card', and that in its turn is explained as consisting of three steps: 'l Write card', 'm Write envelope', 'n Insert card in envelope'. Note that in box (i) it says 'Do a card' not 'Do cards'. The plural is shown by the star in the corner.

Compound conditions

Sometimes a condition is not simple. We buy something if the shop has it AND we have enough money. We wash up if there are dirty pots AND mother (or the boss) says we have to. We go out if it is warm OR the sun is shining. We order more of an item if the level in the warehouse is low AND it is not already on order. We bring in the washing if it rains OR the washing is dry. These are called compound conditions and can easily be used in programs and program designs. On the whole, the way they are made up and the way they work are common sense. They will be discussed in more detail later.

Exercises

Exercises without answers are marked with a *

2.1 Say which of the following is a condition, and where one is not, why.

(a) The ruler is broken.
(b) The scale is metric.
(c) Come to the window.
(d) The people playing the game want another go.
(e) Next Sunday it will rain.
(f) $(3 + 1) < (2 + 2)$
(g) $(4 - 1) + (3 + 2)$
(h) $(3 + 8) >< (6 + 2)$

2.2 Imagine you work in a factory that makes potato crisps, Your job is to take the bags as they come off the production line and pack them into cardboard cartons, which hold 48 bags, for the supermarkets. The diagram should relate to one shift. You pack box after box after box until the end of the shift. To pack a box you do this: put a box in position, fill it, close it and seal it. To fill a box, you pick up a bag and put it in the box until there are 48 in the box. However, if, as you pick up a bag, you notice that it is not sealed properly, you throw it in a reject bin instead of putting it in the box. *Note*: Your diagram should have two repetitions and one selection.

2.3 Oliver goes shopping. Turn the following description into a structure diagram. First he makes a shopping list. He checks he has some money. He goes to town. He visits a number of shops. Each visit involves: walking to the shop, picking up items wanted (a repetitive activity), going to the till, paying, and, finally, checking that he has enough money to continue to the next shop. If he hasn't enough money, he visits the bank. After visiting all the shops, he returns home. *Notes*: The shopping list shows not only what he is going to buy, but also the shops he is going to visit. All the shops are self-service, and what he is going to buy is all straightforward, so he will not have to ask shop assistants for help. The shops always have what he expects them to have.

2.4* Shaving is an activity that involves several repetitions. It is usually done regularly over a period of many years. Every time a bag of razors is used up, another has to be bought. One buys bag after bag after bag. Every two weeks or so a razor becomes too blunt to use. It is discarded and a new one taken from the bag. One uses razor after razor. Every day a razor is used. It is taken from the cupboard, used, rinsed and put back. So each razor is used time after time.

Consider the following activities:

> buying a bag of razors
> opening a bag of razors
> taking a razor from a bag of razors
> taking a razor from the cupboard
> using a razor
> returning a razor to the cupboard
> discarding a razor
> and maybe others

and the following conditions

> the razor is blunt
> the bag is empty
> I have finished shaving (for today)
> I no longer wish to/need to shave

draw a diagram to show a lifetime of shaving.

3

The computer

In the last chapter, everyday situations were used as examples. Now we must move on, to problems that would be suitable for a computer. The problems will have to become more limited and we shall have to deal carefully with details. The real problem for the beginner may be trying to decide what a computer can do and what it cannot. It is because of this that so many teachers of programming start with some actual program writing, and turn to program design later. If you have a teacher or lecturer available, you might try asking for some simple programs to read, in the language you are likely to be using. You could also learn how to use the editor, key in some of the programs and run them. But don't try to write any yet.

A computer is a machine that processes data. You process data too, and so do dogs and other animals. You receive data through your senses of sight, hearing, touch, etc, put it together with facts in your memory, and react – or, in computer terms, produce some output. You may say something or write something or run away or kiss somebody or do any one of a million things. The use of the memory in data processing is very important. People who have almost lost their power to remember, due to an illness such as Alzheimer's disease, need a lot of nursing care because they can no longer function as they used to.

Main memory

Computers have two sorts of store or memory. One is called backing store and on a microcomputer this is usually a disk of some sort. The other is called main memory or RAM (that is, random access memory). This memory is on a chip, is very small, and has no moving parts. The computer can process only the data that is in the main memory. If the data required is only on the backing store, it has to be copied into the main memory before anything can be done with it. The backing store is rather like a book. You cannot use the facts in a book until you have read them – that is, got them into the memory in your brain, even if only for a few minutes. The backing store is like a book you can write in as well as read.

Addresses

Data occupies main memory rather as people occupy towns. In a big city there are tens of thousands of houses, each with its own address. In the same way, in main memory there are hundreds of thousands of **cells** or **locations**, each of which has an address. It is helpful to think of these locations as pigeonholes with labels on.

Figure 3.1 Locations in main memory

| 27 | 28 | The Grange | 30 | Field House | 32 | 33 |

The addresses are really **binary numbers** (that is, numbers made entirely of 1s and 0s), such as 101000101001, but we can use names instead, in our programs. Groups of these cells can be used to hold a word or a sentence or a big number.

Cell names – Variables

One of the really important things a program does is to reserve cells in main memory for the various items of data that it is going to process, give them names, and say what kind of data is going to be stored there. There are basically two kinds of data: **numeric**, which can be used for arithmetic, and **non-numeric**, but at this early stage we shall not have to worry about that. The names are chosen by the programmer, and it is a great help if each name indicates clearly what the cell is to be used for. Examples of names that might be used are: page_number, quantity_in_stock, and date_of_birth. The named cells are usually called **identifiers** or **variables** or **data-names** or **fields**. With a few exceptions, the word used in this book will be **variable**.

Statements

Having allocated memory – that is, named the locations needed for the data – the program gets data into some of these locations, manipulates it, and then outputs some results. The programmer makes all this happen by writing **statements**. For our program designs we need only three or four different kinds of statement. They are named and described below. The ones chosen do not relate to any programming language in particular.

In the descriptions two **verbs** will be used: to **input** and to **output**. If you are new to computers the use of these words as verbs may seem odd, but you will soon get used to it. Where in common speech we might say, 'The clerk fed in some data and the computer produced some results', in this jargon we say, 'The clerk input some data and the computer output some results'.

READ

The read statement gets, or tries to get, data from an input device. This may be a keyboard, a disk drive, a bar-code scanner, a pressure gauge or some other device, but to begin with will be the keyboard. The format of the READ statement will be

READ variable...

This is read as the key word READ followed by the name of a storage location that was allocated earlier. The three dots mean that other variable names may follow. Each item of data to be keyed in is to be stored in the locations named. For example,

```
Read name,
address
```

will cause a pause, while the computer waits for the user to key in a name. As soon as they do, it will be stored in the location called 'name'. What the user keys in next will be stored in the location called 'address'.

WRITE

The write statement causes data to be copied to an output device. This may be a screen, a printer, a plotter, a motor, or some other device. To begin with it will be the screen. Before we look at the format of the statement a new word will have to be introduced: **literal**. A literal is a number or word that appears in the program and is used or output exactly as it stands. Non-numeric literals go in quotes. Some programming languages use double quotes (") and others use single quotes ('). We shall use singles. A nonnumeric literal does not have to be a word; it can be any collection of characters. Examples of literals are: 35, 'Press any key to continue', 3.142, '£ '. Note that in the last example, the literal is two characters: a £ sign followed by a space. The format of the WRITE statement will be

WRITE $\left\{ \begin{array}{l} \text{variable} \\ \text{literal} \end{array} \right\}$ ...

The curly brackets indicate a choice, so this is read as the key word WRITE, followed by either the name of a storage location that was allocated earlier, or a literal. The three dots mean that other variable names and/or literals may follow. Each item of data to be written is to be copied from the locations named. For example,

```
Write account_
number, amount
```

will cause the contents of the locations called account_number and amount to be displayed on the screen.

LET

The main processing statement will be the LET statement. It will have two formats.

Format 1 $\text{LET variable-1} = \begin{Bmatrix} \text{variable-2} \\ \text{literal} \end{Bmatrix}$

The effect of the format 1 let is that the contents of variable-2 (or the literal) are copied into variable-1. If variable-2 is used, its contents are unchanged. For example suppose a variable named prize contains zero, and a second variable named total_collected contains 150000. Then

```
Let prize =
total_collected
```

will cause 150000 to be copied into prize, so that now, both total_collected and prize contain 150000. Another example would be

```
Let announcement =
'total collected'
```

This would cause the words 'total collected' to be placed in the variable called announcement. Whatever announcement had in it before would be lost. The variable on the left of the equals sign is sometimes called the **receiving field** or the **destination** or the **target**.

Format 2   LET variable = arithmetic expression

Arithmetic expression

The arithmetic expression can be any piece of arithmetic or algebra that can be worked out. The computer puts the result of the working-out into variable. The arithmetic expression could be something very simple such as 2 + 2, or something more complicated such as

$$((pay - allowance / 12) - pension)/(1 / tax\_rate)$$

In these expressions,

add is shown by +
subtract by   −
multiply by   *
divide by   /

The asterisk, *, is used to show multiplication, because there is no little cross on a keyboard, and x would be taken as a letter. The divide sign of a dash with a dot above it and a dot below it is also not available on a keyboard. Fractions written on two lines, e.g. $\frac{1}{2}$, $\frac{1}{4}$ would be very awkward to type, so the slash, /, is used instead, as in the example above. Programming languages require that the assumed multiplication between a variable and an opening bracket is made explicit, so that computer programmers write y*(1+r) not y(1+r).

It is important to note that

LET total_goals = total_goals + 1

makes sense. Total_goals is the name of a location in main store. Suppose it contains 3. The instruction causes the arithmetic 3 + 1 to be done and the result, 4, to be stored in the location called total_goals. The symbol '=', as it is used here, does not mean 'equals', it means 'become equal to'.

ADD

Because adding numbers will crop up often, and using LET to do addition is rather clumsy, a fourth type of statement, ADD, will be used. The format is:

ADD $\left\{ \begin{array}{l} \text{variable-1} \\ \text{literal} \end{array} \right\}$ TO variable-2

The result replaces the original value in variable-2. The contents of variable-1 are unchanged.

Examples are:

add tax to net_pay
add 1 to counter

An adding program

With these four types of statement, read, write, let and add, a great many programs can be designed. Because a computer, as it stands, cannot even do addition like a calculator, a useful first program would be one to add up a list of numbers. Let us start by thinking how we would do it if we had no computer or calculator. If we had single digit numbers like 3, 5 and 8, we would write them all down in a column, add them up, and write down the answer. It would be possible to get the computer to work like that, but there would be snags. Fig. 3.2 shows a design for three numbers.

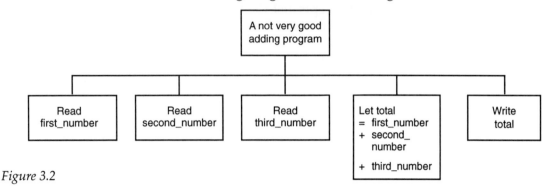

Figure 3.2

You should now attempt Exercise 3.1 at the end of the chapter.

There are two obvious problems with the diagram for addition shown in Fig. 3.2. The let box is too big and too full. If there were 10 numbers instead of 3, the diagram would be very clumsy, and tedious to draw. Both these problems can be overcome by writing the actions in a numbered list, and using thinner boxes, as below:

Action list
1.   read first_number
2.   read second_number
3.   read third_number
4.   read fourth_number
     ...and so on to
10. read tenth_number
11. let total = first_number + second_number + third_number + fourth_number ..... + tenth_number
12. write total

See Fig. 3.3.

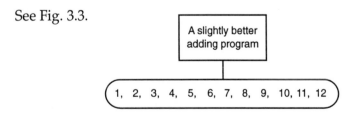

Figure 3.3

That is much better, and from now on action lists will be used, and the numbers for actions will go in shallow boxes with curved ends, which in this book will be called lozenges. However, the solution is still clumsy. There are a lot of actions for such a simple problem. Action 11 is very long. More importantly, we need to know how many numbers the user wants to add up, before we do the design and write the program. Can you imagine a calculator where, before you could add up 15 numbers, you had to load the program that accepts just 15 numbers?! It would be better if the user could first enter the length of the list of numbers to be added, and then have the adding within a part of the program that is repeated. Using such a repetition, or iteration, a new, better design can be produced, but some new variables will be needed. The variables used before were First_number, Second_number etc., and Total. First_number, Second_number etc., will all be replaced by the single variable called *Number. Total* will still be needed. The number of numbers to be added will need to be kept somewhere. We shall store that in an variable called *List_length*. The numbers, as they are read and added in, will be counted. The number showing the state of the count will be held in the variable called *Counter*.

It would have been handy if the names of the variables we shall need had been jotted down as we saw the need for them, to form a list. If that had been done we should have had the following:

Variable list

number	a number to be added
list_length	the number of numbers to be expected
counter	the number of numbers dealt with so far
total	the total so far

The new action list will be:

Action list

1. write 'How many numbers are there? '
2. read list_length
3. let counter = 0
4. let total = 0
5. write 'Key in a number '
6. read number
7. let total = total + number (or, add number to total)
8. add 1 to counter
9. write 'The total is ', total

The resulting diagram is shown in Fig. 3.4.

The names 'Main' and 'Get & tally' are invented so that each part of the diagram can be referred to. They need to be short and also give some indication of what that part of the diagram does. 'Main' is the main part of the program, between the preliminaries (actions 1,2,3,4) and the bit at the end

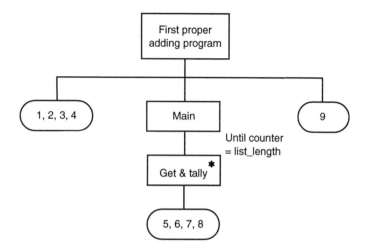

Figure 3.4

(action 9). 'Get & tally' indicates what happens at this point: we get some data and do some adding. This is more precisely defined by actions 5,6,7,8. Because 'Get & tally' has a star in the top right corner, it and everything below it, is repeated until *Counter* becomes equal to *List_length*

Note that if the diagram is seen as an upside-down tree, like a family tree, the lozenges are the tips of the branches. A lozenge full of actions cannot be broken down into anything simpler; therefore it should never have anything hanging from it.

To see how this design works, suppose the list of numbers to be added is 8, 5, 2. After actions 1, 2, 3 and 4 the cells in main memory named by our variables have these values:

number = 0,
list_length = 3,
counter = 0 and
total = 0.

The condition 'counter = list_length' is not true, so the repetition is entered, and 5, 6, 7 and 8 are done. Now

number = 8,
list_length = 3,
counter = 1 and
total = 8

The condition 'counter = list_length' is still not true, so the repetition is re-entered, and 5, 6, 7 and 8 are done again. Now

number = 5,
list_length = 3,
counter = 2 and
total = 13

The condition 'counter = list_length' is still not true, so the repetition is re-entered, and 5, 6, 7 and 8 are done again. Now

number = 2,
list_length = 3,
counter = 3 and
total = 15

The condition 'counter = list_length' is now true, the repetition is over, and control goes to action 9. The total, 15, is displayed and the program stops.

If there were a lot of numbers to be added, it might be an annoying extra task to count up how many there were before starting to key them in, and if you miscounted, it would be awkward. An alternative is to end the list with a number that is kept specially for that purpose, acts as a marker, and is not added in. If numbers as big as 999999 were never going to appear in the list to be added, 999999 would do. If negative numbers were never going to appear in the list, –1 would do. A value used as a marker in this way is called a **rogue value** or **dummy value**. Here is an alternative design for a program that adds a list of numbers, using –1 as a rogue value.

Only two locations in main store are needed, one to hold the number just keyed in, and one to hold the total so far.

Variable list

| number | (for the number just keyed in) |
| total | (for the total so far) |

Action list

1. let total = 0
2. write 'Key in a number '
3. read number
4. add number to total
5. write 'The total is ', total

For the diagram, see Fig. 3.5.

To see how this works, suppose the list of numbers to be added is 8, 5, 2, with –1 at the end. After actions 1, 2 and 3, before the repetition has started,

number = 8,
total = 0.

The condition 'number = –1' is not true, so the repetition is entered, and 4, 2 and 3 are done, in that order. Now

number = 5,
total = 8.

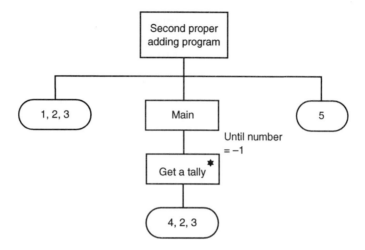

Figure 3.5

The condition 'number = –1' is still not true, so the repetition is re-entered, and 4, 2 and 3 are done again. Now

number = 2,
total = 13.

The condition 'number = –1' is still not true, so the repetition is re-entered, and 4, 2 and 3 are done again. Now

number = –1
total = 15

The condition 'number = –1' is now true, the repetition is over, and control goes to action 5. The total, 15, is displayed and the program stops.

As you see, there are fewer variables and fewer actions, so, in a way, the design is neater.

At this point you could attempt Exercise 3.2 at the end of the chapter.

Processing words

Computers, as we know, can do more than arithmetic, they can process words as well. The reason is that all characters, whether they are digits or letters or special characters (such as *, > and %) are held inside the computer as binary numbers. In many computers, A is stored and moved about as 1000001, B as 1000010, an exclamation mark, !, as 0100101 and a blank space as 0100000. The codes for the letters get bigger as the letters get nearer the end of the alphabet. Note that, for the time being, all reference to letters will be to capitals. Bringing in lower case letters at this point would complicate matters.

The way the computer works helps us with words in another way. Not only is B bigger than A, but CUT is bigger than CAT, because U is bigger than A. Note that CUT is also bigger than CATASTROPHE, because U is bigger than A. Put another way, the condition, 'CUT' > 'CATASTROPHE' is TRUE. This enables us to design programs involving words. We are now going to design a program that accepts two words from the keyboard and prints them in **alphabetical** order. To do this, a selection will be used, as was explained on page 3 of Chapter 2.

Two locations in main store will be needed, one for each of the words. These will be called Word_1 and Word_2

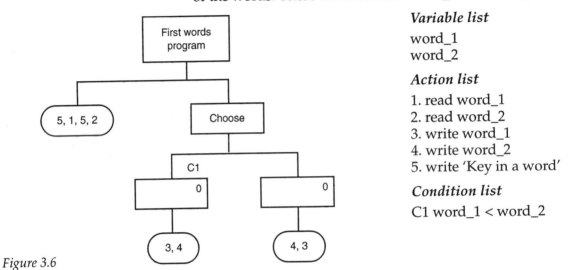

Variable list

word_1
word_2

Action list

1. read word_1
2. read word_2
3. write word_1
4. write word_2
5. write 'Key in a word'

Condition list

C1 word_1 < word_2

Figure 3.6

Several general points are worth noting here.

- A condition list has been used, instead of putting the condition directly on the diagram.
- The order in which actions appear in the action list has nothing to do with the order in which they appear on the diagram.
- The order in which actions appear on the diagram is very important.
- Any action in the action list can appear more than once on the diagram.
- The condition boxes are not on the same line as the lozenge with 5,1,5,2 in it. Sequence boxes and condition boxes should not be mixed.

With two words, there are two possible orders: first, second or second, first. With three words, there are six possible orders:

1st, 2nd, 3rd	2nd, 3rd, 1st
1st, 3rd, 2nd	3rd, 1st, 2nd
2nd, 1st, 3rd	3rd, 2nd, 1st.

As a result, a program to accept three words and print them

in alphabetical order will be a lot more complicated. Here is a solution. It assumes that all the words are different (and all in capital letters). Fig. 3.7 shows the result.

Variable list	*Action list*
word_1	1. write word_1
word_2	2. write word_2
word_3	3. write word_3
	4. read word_1
Condition list	5. read word_2
C1 word_1 < word_2	6. read word_3
C2 word_1 < word_3	7. write 'Key a word'
C3 word_2 < Word_3	

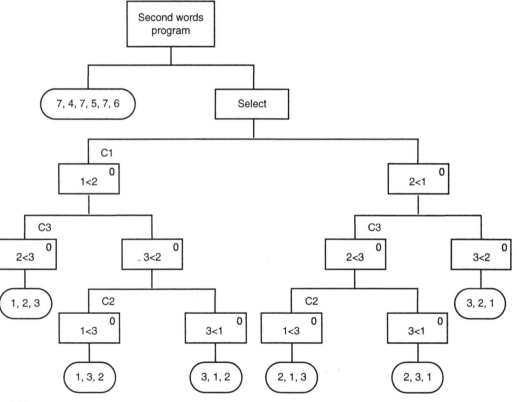

Figure 3.7

There are many solutions to this problem. Here is another. The variable list and action list are as before.

Condition list

C1 word_1 < word_2 AND word_2 < word_3
C2 word_1 < word_3 AND word_3 < word_2
C3 word_2 < word_3 AND word_3 < word_1

C4 word_2 < word_1 AND word_1 < word_3
C5 word_3 < word_1 AND word_1 < word_2
C6 word_3 < word_2 AND word_2 < word_1

The diagram is shown in Fig. 3.8.

Which of the two is better is probably just a matter of taste. It may be that you prefer simple conditions and a complex diagram, or you may prefer compound conditions and simple diagram. Which is easier to code may depend on the programming language you use. How would you put four words into alphabetical order? There are 24 possibilities. How about ten words? There are 3 628 800 possibilities. Happily, in Chapter 6, we shall see that there is a way of doing it without drawing three million boxes.

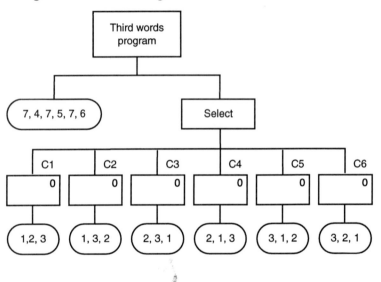

Figure 3.8

Exercises

Exercises without answers are marked with a *.

3.1 Design a program to accept two numbers from a keyboard and subtract the second from the first.

3.2 A beginner attempted to simplify the addition design which has −1 to mark the end of the data. He used the same variable list and action list as on page 20, but used the diagram shown in Fig. 3.9. Explain what is wrong with this design.

3.3 Design a program to accept two numbers from a keyboard and subtract the smaller from the larger.

3.4 Design a program that will add or subtract, using two numbers. First it prompts the user for two numbers. Then it asks the user whether to add or subtract. The user replies either 'A' for add or 'S' for subtract. The program does as required. Note. Do not try to deal with the problem of what would happen if the user keyed neither 'A' nor 'S'. This refinement, which is called validation, will be dealt with in a later chapter.

3.5* Design a program that will accept a list of numbers, the length of which is not known, and print both the total and the average. (The average is the total divided by the number of numbers in the list.)

3.6 Design a program that will accept three numbers, all different, and then print them in order, with the largest first.

3.7 Check your answer to question 3.6 to see if it would work if two of the numbers were the same. If it would not, produce a design for a program that would.

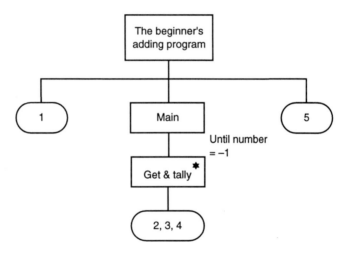

Figure 3.9

4

Repeats of repeats – having another go

Repeat and Iterate
In other books about program design you may see the word **iterate** used where this book uses the word repeat. Iterate is a word used by mathematicians and it means repeat. In program design the two words are interchangeable.

The program on pages 18 and 19 did simple adding up, like a calculator, but when it had printed the answer, it stopped. If you wanted to add up another column of figures, you had to restart it, or, to use the jargon, **execute** it again. This is awkward for the person who is going to use the program (the **user**). It would be better if the user were asked if they would like another go. We shall look now at the changes needed to achieve this.

The variable list needs a new entry, shown in italics here:

Variable list

number
list-length
counter
total
again

'Again' will be used to store a single character (Y or N). This will show whether the user wants to use the program again, to add up another list of figures, or not. It will be **initialized** to 'Y', i.e. given the value 'Y', standing for YES, at the beginning, to make sure that the main part of the program will execute at least once. After the writing of the result it will be prompted for, and the user will, we hope, key either 'Y' or 'N' into it. In practice, the user may make a mistake and key something else, such as 'OK' or 'QUIT'. To avoid the complications of displaying error messages, the program will take anything other than plain 'N' to mean yes, and repeat.

The action list, therefore, needs three new entries, again shown in italics:

Action list

1. write 'How many numbers are there? '

2. read list-length
3. let counter = 0
4. let total = 0
5. write 'Key in a number '
6. read number
7. let total = total + number
8. let counter = counter + 1
9. write 'The total is ', total
10. *write 'Another go? (Y/N) ' (The user is asked to key either Y for YES or N for NO)*
11. *read again*
12. *let again = 'Y'*

The diagram is shown in Fig. 4.1.

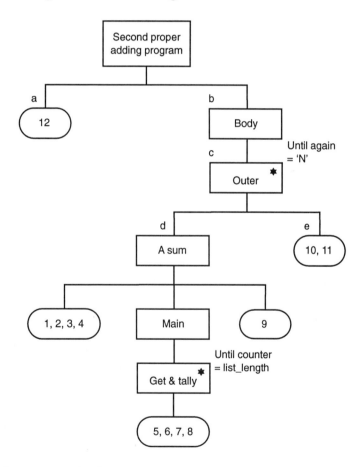

Figure 4.1

The part marked a to e is a new insertion. The names 'Body', 'A sum' etc. are not important. They are invented so that each part of the diagram can be referred to.

There are two repetition boxes now. One hangs below, and is therefore a part of, the other. 'Get & tally' repeats within 'A sum', and 'A sum' repeats within 'Body'. We see this kind of thing in clocks: seconds repeat within minutes and minutes repeat within hours. Minutes repeat until the hour is complete, and then they start to repeat again inside the new hour. In the diagram above, numbers are prompted for and obtained until one addition is complete and the answer displayed; the repeated prompting and obtaining then starts again, for the next sum.

The situation above is sometimes called a 'nested repetition', and sometimes called a 'loop within a loop'.

You should now attempt Exercise 4.1.

Ending a repetition

Repetitions that just go on and on until someone switches the computer off are occasionally used, but normally they are ended by a particular event or value. In theory the repetition of a sequence of statements could be abandoned at any point in the sequence, but in practice it has been found that such freedom leads to programs that are very difficult to read. It is hard to correct errors in such programs and hard to alter them when they need to be brought up to date. There is therefore a rule that the test for the terminating event or value is always made either *just before* the repeated code is entered or *just after* its end is reached. These are sometimes referred to as 'while loops' and 'until loops', but such terms can be confusing because what they mean can depend on the programming language being used.

There are really four possibilities:

1. **Test before.**   Exit repetition when condition is false.
2. **Test before.**   Exit repetition when condition is true.
3. **Test after.**   Exit repetition when condition is false.
4. **Test after.**   Exit repetition when condition is true.

Examples

Of 1: WHILE condition DO , in Pascal.
　　　　WHILE condition, in C.
　　　　WHILE condition, in some versions of Basic.
Of 2: PERFORM WITH TEST BEFORE UNTIL condition, in COBOL.
Of 3: DO statement WHILE condition, in C
Of 4: REPEAT statement UNTIL condition, in Pascal.
　　　　REPEAT/UNTIL, in many versions of Basic.
　　　　PERFORM WITH TEST AFTER UNTIL condition, in COBOL.

When the test is made after, the block of code to be repeated is always executed at least once. When the test is made before, it may not be executed at all. *Test before* is therefore more versatile, but the code that gives *test after* may be easier to write correctly and easier to read.

In the designs in this book, from here on, only types 1, 2 and 4 will be used, and they will be distinguished as follows. The condition itself will be put in a Condition list. Words will be used on the diagram, with the reference to the list, as shown in Fig. 4.2.

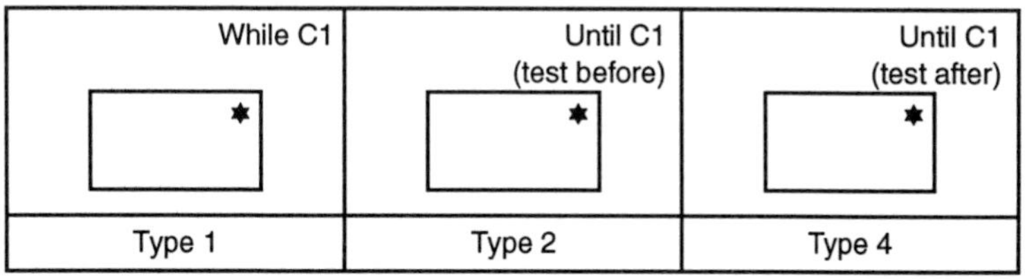

While C1	Until C1 (test before)	Until C1 (test after)
∗	∗	∗
Type 1	Type 2	Type 4

Figure 4.2

The repetition 'Get & tally' in figure 4.1 could be either type 2 or type 4, the only difference being that if listlength were input as zero (unlikely), and it were of type 4, the user would be prompted for a number they didn't have. To make it a type 1, the condition would have to be changed so that next to the asterisk we had 'While counter < listlength'.

It is usually easy to get the control of the repetition *nearly* right. It is often much more difficult to get it *exactly* right, and of course it must be exactly right if the program is to be satisfactory. The condition and the way it is tested may depend on what initialization is done. Before that is investigated, it is necessary to look at a way of finding out whether a design is exactly right or not.

Note that the opposite of > is <=, and the opposite of < is >=. If > and < are treated as opposites, the equal situation may be missed. For example, if the variable w_quantity contains the value 4, then the conditions (w_quantity > 4) and (w_quantity < 4) are both FALSE.

> **Initialization** is the assignation of a value to a variable either at the beginning of a program or the beginning of a part of a program.

Dry running

With a good deal of practice, you will be able to check small parts of your designs in your head, but to begin with, and in tricky situations, it is necessary to write down the steps, using a pencil and paper. It is also necessary to label all the boxes. As an example, the design at the beginning of this chapter will be used.

The condition list is:

C1 again = 'N'
C2 counter = list-length

The diagram is shown in Fig. 4.3.
Next, decide on a small amount of data. We shall have: three

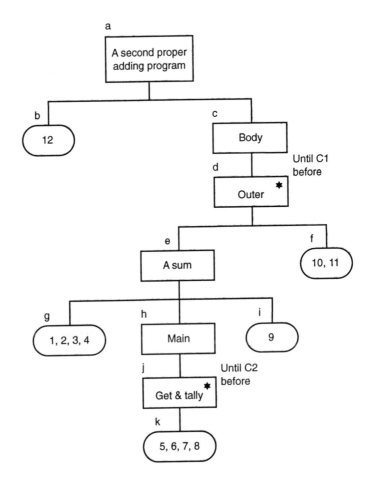

Figure 4.3

numbers, 7, 3 and 2. Then, to the prompt of 'more?' we shall answer Y, and follow with two more numbers, 47 and 53. On the next prompt of 'more?' the answer will be N.

Columns must be ruled for the steps, the variables, the conditions, and the outcome. The first line will show the initial states of all the variables, in this case, unknown

Step	Number	List Length	Counter	Total	Again	C1	C2	Outcome
(1)	?	?	?	?	?	?	?	

The diagram is then followed through, box by box, including the lozenges, and every time a variable or condition changes, this is recorded, against it, in the appropriate column. The result for this example is shown in Fig. 4.4. A step is shown in brackets if its influence is solely via the refinement below it.

Step	Number	List Length	Counter	Total	Again	C1	C2	Outcome
(a)	?	?	?	?	?	?	?	
b					Y			
(c)								
d						False		
e								
g		3	0	0				
(h)								
j							False	
k	7		1	7				
j							False	
k	3		2	10				
j							False	
k	2		3	12				
j							True	
k								12
f					Y			
d						False		
(e)								
g		2	0	0				
(h)								
j							False	
k	47		1	47				
j							False	
k	53		2	100				
j							True	
i								100
f					N			
d						True		
	d is now complete, which completes c, which completes a and ends the program.							

Figure 4.4

Translation into code

A design is only useful if it can easily be translated into code, of course. This book is not about any particular programming language, but in order to illustrate how the designs can be turned into programs, the design given at the beginning of this chapter, called 'Second proper adding program' will now be coded in C, Pascal, Cobol-85 and Basic. Only minimal facilities of the languages will be used, partly because if you are learning a language at the same time as using this book, you will know only a little of it at this stage. In particular there is no parameter passing.

C

The following translations are used:

- Read becomes either scanf or getche. Since getche is a function that returns a single character, Read *again* becomes again = getche().
- Write becomes printf.
- Let is unchanged except that the word Let itself is dropped.
- Because the While statements show the condition for the repetition to continue as opposed to the condition for the repetition to stop, they will have to be reversed or almost so. The first condition, Again = 'N' becomes Again != 'N', and the second condition, Counter = list_length becomes Counter < list_length.

Extra to the actions in the list are the statements Return() at the ends of the functions. This is required by the way C works.

```c
/* C (Turbo C) */
#include <stdio.h>
int w_list_length, w_number, w_total;
int w_counter;
char w_again;

/* The algorithm shown in the diagram starts
here. */
void main()
{
 w_again = 'Y';
 while (w_again != 'N')
 {
     outer();
     printf("\nAnother go (Y/N) ");
     w_again = getche();
 }
}
outer()
{
 printf("\nHow many numbers are there? ");
 scanf("%d",&w_list_length);
 w_counter=0; w_total=0;
 while (w_counter < w_list_length)
     get_and_tally();
 printf("\nThe total is %d",w_total);
 return(0);
}
```

```
get_and_tally()
{
 printf("\nKey in a number ");
 scanf("%d",&w_number);
 w_total = w_total + w_number;
 w_counter++;
 return(0);
}
/* *** End of  C  code  *************/
```

Pascal

- Write sometimes codes as WRITE and sometimes as WRITELN.
- Read codes directly as READLN.
- The Let actions are changed by the dropping of the word Let, and the insertion of a colon before the equals sign, so Let again = 'Y' becomes again := 'Y'.
- The conditions use WHILE and so must be changed exactly as in 'C' above, except that not equals is coded <> instead of !=. Uniquely, Pascal has to be coded from the bottom up, which is all right once you are used to it!

```
{Pascal}
PROGRAM second_proper_adding_program;
VAR
w_list_length, w_number, w_total :INTEGER;
w_counter: INTEGER;
w_again: CHAR;
{The algorithm in the diagram starts here,
but at the bottom.}
PROCEDURE get_and_tally;
BEGIN
 WRITE('Key in a number ');
 READLN(w_number);
 w_total:=w_total+w_number;
 w_counter:=w_counter+1
END;
PROCEDURE outer;
BEGIN
 WRITE('How many numbers are there? ');
 READLN(w_list_length);
 w_total:=0; w_counter:=0;
 WHILE w_counter < w_list_length DO
     get_and_tally;
 WRITELN('The total is ', w_total);
END;
{This is the top of the diagram. In Pascal it
comes at the end.}
```

```
BEGIN
 w_again := 'Y';
 WHILE w_again <> 'N' DO
      BEGIN
      outer;
      WRITE('Another go? (Y/N) ');
      READLN(w_again)
      END
END.
{***** end of Pascal code *************}
```

Cobol-85

As this program does not handle files, but uses just screen
and keyboard, the following translations will be needed:

- Write will become Display.
- Read will become Accept.
- Let will become Move, and reversed. For example,
      Let total = 0 becomes
      Move 0 to total.

To avoid the use of reserved words, all variables will be prefixed by w-. Because in standard Cobol, Accept is very
primitive, it will be assumed that the user will always key
two digits when asked for a number and will key in leading
zeros where necessary. The chapter on validation will show
how these restrictions can be avoided. The output is not zero-
suppressed because that would require procedure division
statements not shown in the design.

```
*** Cobol-85 ***
 identification division.
 program-id. second-proper-adding-program.
 data division.
 working-storage section.
 1    in-out.
     5 w-list-length  pic 99.
     5 w-number        pic 99.
     5 w-total         pic 9999.
 1    repeat-controls.
     5 w-counter       pic 99.
     5 w-again         pic x.

*** The algorithm shown in the diagram starts here ***
 procedure division.
     move "Y" to w-again
     perform until w-again = "N"
        perform outer
```

```
        display "Another go? (Y/N) " with no advancing
        accept w-again
    end-perform
    stop run.
outer.
    display "How many numbers are there? " with
        no advancing
    accept w-list-length
    move 0 to w-counter, w-total
    perform get-and-tally until w-counter = w-list-length
    display "The total is "w-total.
get-and-tally.
    display "Key in a number " with no advancing
    accept w-number
    add w-number to w-total
    add 1 to w-counter.
**** END OF COBOL CODE *****************
```

Basic

```
BASIC
10 REM  BASIC
15 REM  The algorithm shown in the diagram
starts right here!
20 LET wagain$ = "Y"
30 WHILE wagain$ <> "N"
40   GOSUB 80:  REM outer
50   PRINT ("Another go? (Y/N) ");
55   INPUT wagain$
60 WEND
70 END
80 REM outer
90 PRINT ("How many numbers are there? ");
100 INPUT wlistlength
110 LET wcounter = 0: LET wtotal = 0
120 WHILE wcounter <> wlistlength
130   GOSUB 200:   REM get-and-tally
140 WEND
150 PRINT ("The total is ");
160 PRINT (wtotal)
170 RETURN
200 REM get-and-tally
210 PRINT ("Key in a number ");
220 INPUT wnumber
230 LET wtotal = wtotal + wnumber
240 LET wcounter = wcounter + 1
250 RETURN
260 REM **** end of BASIC code
***********************
```

Reversal of conditions

In the diagrams, the type 2 control has been used on the repetition: Test before and exit when condition is true. This has been done because it seems more natural and obvious. To write the code it is often necessary to change this to type 1 control: Test before and exit when condition is false. This means reversing the condition. You should note the following:

- The opposite of = is <> or NOT = or !=
- The opposite of > is <=
- The opposite of < is >=
- The opposite of >= is <
- The opposite of <= is >

Example

A design uses the variable Counter and says, 'Go on repeating until counter > 20'. This may have to be changed to something like, 'Go on repeating while counter <= 20'.

With compound conditions it is necessary to change not only the operators but the also the AND or OR.

- The opposite of AND is OR
- The opposite of OR is AND

Example

A design uses the variables x and y, and says, 'Go on repeating until x > 20 OR y = 0.' This may have to be changed to something like 'Go on repeating while x <= 20 AND y <> 0.'

Exercises

There are no answers at the end of the book for questions marked *

4.1 Modify the first of the two designs in chapter 3 that put three words in order (Fig. 3.7), so that the user can go on supplying sets of three words as many times as wished.

4.2 Modify your answer to Exercise 3.3 so that the user can repeatedly get subtractions done.

4.3 Produce complete dry runs for the designs you produced in answer to Exercises 4.1 and 4.2.

4.4 Alter the design of Fig. 4.3 so that it uses WHILE on both conditions, instead of UNTIL.

4.5* Design a program to calculate how a capital sum of money increases in value over a period of years. It should accept input of

(a) a capital sum
(b) a rate of interest
(c) a number of years

The outputs should be a heading that restates the inputs, followed by a list showing the value of the capital at the end of each year.

4.6* Design a program to do this: print a table of the value of a capital sum of money when saved at 3, 6, 9, 12 and 15% over a period of 20 years, in steps of two years. The appearance of the results should be similar to this:

AMOUNT = 2000

AT	3%	6%	9%	12%	15%
AFTER years					
2	2122	2247	2376	2509	2645
4	2251	2525			
6	2388				
8	2534				

....

and so on

4.7* A shop is having a knock-down sale. New LOW prices are worked out as follows, on ex-vat prices.

1. Everything is first reduced by a fixed amount, according to category.
   Category C, children's, reduced by £1
   Category W, women's, reduced by £3
   Category M, men's, reduced by £2
   Category U, unisex, reduced by £4
2. Then, everything has a fixed 12% knocked off.
3. Then, VAT is added, at 20% (even children's) and new price tickets are made out.

Design a program that will read a description, category and old-price, ex-vat, and print a ticket with the description and new selling price. For example, if 'FROCK', 'W', 10 is keyed in, the label

| Frock   £7.08 |

should be printed

A description of 'XXX' should end the program.

4.8* Extend the design of Exercise 4.7 as follows. A summary should print at the end of the run, showing

(a) totals of prices keyed in, by category
(b) totals of the new prices (before VAT is added) by category
(c) the 'losses', by category
(d) the total 'loss'.

Example (The figures are for illustration only)

	Children's	Women's	Men's	Unisex
Old totals	23.00	86.50	92.60	47.25
New totals	18.50	63.75	74.20	31.00
Losses	4.50	22.75	18.40	16.25

Total loss   61.90

5

Menus and subroutines

In this chapter we shall see how to incorporate a menu into a program. We shall also see that most programs can usefully be broken down into parts, called subprograms or subroutines. But first we will look at another little topic: data types.

Data types

It was mentioned in chapter 3 that when a cell in main store is named by a variable, the coding in the program will also indicate whether the cell is to contain numeric or non-numeric data. This gives the data-item or variable a **type**. The programmer has to give an item the type **numeric** if it will be necessary to do arithmetic with it. Otherwise an item is given a **non-numeric** type. A number with which we would never do arithmetic, such as a telephone number, would usually be given the type non-numeric.

All programming languages distinguish between whole numbers (**integers**) and those that have a decimal point (e.g. **real** in Pascal and **float** in C). Such a distinction will seldom be necessary in this book.

Although in all programming languages the main division is between numeric and non-numeric, many other types are possible. In this book we shall consider only two others, character and boolean.

Character

If a non-numeric item is of length one, that is to say the location in main store is to hold only one character, the type may be character.

Boolean

The funny name comes from a mathematician called George

Boole. The idea is very simple, and is connected with conditions. A boolean item is one that can have one of just two values: TRUE or FALSE. In fact, in the inside of the computer, it is probably just one bit, and is either 1 or 0, but in this book the values TRUE and FALSE will be used.

The boolean type is usually used for **flags**. A flag is a variable that is used to show whether something is true or false, or whether an event has happened or not, or whether some item is present or not. For example a boolean item may show whether the end of a file has been reached or whether a member of the club has paid his/her subscription or not.

As it is necessary to avoid attempting to do arithmetic with non-numeric items, it may be useful to indicate a variable's type when writing the variable list. The following symbols will be used from now on:

N to indicate numeric
X to indicate non-numeric
T to indicate boolean
C to indicate character (just one character)

If it is necessary to distinguish between numeric integers and numeric-with-decimal, the codes NI for integer and ND for decimal, will be used.

Menus

Before the days of menus, the computer user was presented with questions like, 'What do you want?'. The user had to know what was available. If they didn't, it meant consulting a manual. The answer was often a code word, and had to be spelt exactly as given. Little mistakes meant a lot of frustration. Now, the choices are listed, and it may be possible to make the choice with a mouse.

The use of a mouse and other aspects of what is known as a 'graphical interface' are too advanced for this book, but simple menus, from which the user chooses by keying the initial letter of a phrase, or a number, can easily be incorporated into simple programs and simple designs.

In the most basic case the program contains just **one menu**. This will be illustrated with an example which looks rather silly, but that is because the choices themselves are unimportant just now. What matters at the moment is how the choices are made.

Example

A very simple computer in a place where computers are being demonstrated is to be programmed so that users are presented with the following options:

1. Have a name printed on screen 20 times
2. Display a message for boyfriend or girlfriend
3. Show whether a number is more or less than 16
4. Tell you whether you are fat, thin, or just right.

The user is prompted to key the initial letter, H, D, S or T. There is another option, which is not listed:

5. End the program

This choice is for the use of the people who set up the computer, so they can close the program down before they go home. It is hoped that members of the public will not key 'E' by mistake!

At the end of each of the four main activities there will be the prompt, 'Press Enter to return to the menu'.

The beginning of one possible design would be:

> **Reminder**
>
> A Variable list names locations in main store. It states how many storage locations the program needs, and gives them names. It may also indicate what data-type the data stored there will have.

Variable list

choice. One alphanumeric character.

Action list

1. Write the menu (note that this is several statements).
2. Write the prompt 'Key an initial letter, H, D, S or T'.
3. Read choice.

Condition list

C1 choice = 'E'
C2 choice = 'H'
C3 choice = 'D'
C4 choice = 'S'
C5 choice = 'T'   See Fig. 5.1

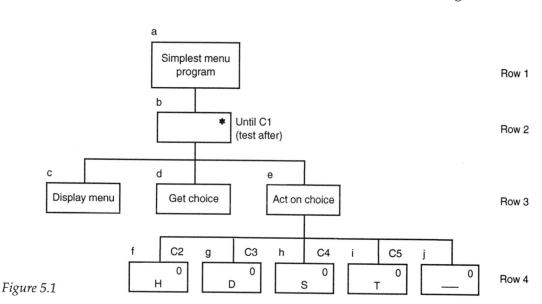

Figure 5.1

Reminder

A dash like the one in box j means 'do nothing'.

The H in box f means 'Have name printed on screen 20 times', the D in box g means 'Display message for...' and so on.

When the programs starts, control goes straight to box c because the test on the repetition is done at the end of it.

The **refinement** of c is:

c

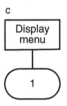

The refinement of d is:

d

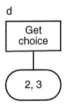

If the choice is H, D, S or T, the activity requested happens, and in each case is completed when the user responds to a prompt, 'Press Enter to return to the menu'. If the choice is anything else, row 4, and hence box e, is immediately complete. Row 3 being complete, the condition on the repetition is tested. If the variable *Choice* contains 'E', box b is complete, box a is complete and the program terminates. Otherwise, the repeat is activated, and control passes again to box c, so the menu is re-displayed.

A convention

From here on, when a variable that is in a variable list is referred to in an explanation nearby, it will start with a capital letter and be in italics.

The refinements of the individual activities, H, D, S and T are unimportant, but they are developed below for the sake of completeness.

H

For '1, Have a name displayed 20 times', three new variables will be introduced:

Variable list continued

j   numeric, to act as a counter,
k   non-numeric, for anything keyed in response to
         the request for Enter,
name   for the name keyed in.

A design would be

Action list continued

4. write prompt for name
5. read name
6. let j = 1
7. write 'Press Enter to return to the menu'
8. read k (and Enter)
9. write name
10. add 1 to j.

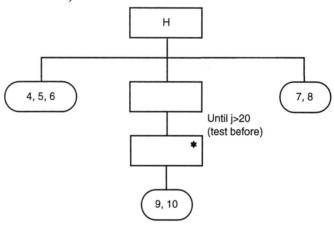

Figure 5.2

D

For '2. Display a message for boyfriend or girlfriend', the user will be prompted for his/her own name, e.g. George, and the friend's name, e.g. Mavis. The variables for these will be *Name-own* and *Name-other*. A message such as 'Mavis, I love you - be mine for ever - George' will display, (the names used being those keyed). Except for the names, the message will always be the same. The design is similar to the one above, but simpler.

Action list continued

11. write prompt for name-own
12. read name-own
13. write prompt for name-other
14. read name-other
15. write name-other, ', I love you - be mine for ever - ', name-own.

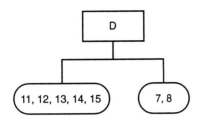

Figure 5.3

Also needed are two actions used before,

7.   write 'Press Enter to return to the menu'
8.   read k (and Enter)

See Fig. 5.3.

S

For '3. Show whether a number is more or less than 16', the user will be prompted for a number. What is input will be tested to see if it is numeric, and the prompt repeated if it is not. It will then be tested and a message printed. The variable *Num* will be used for the number.

Action list continued for S

16. write prompt 'Key in your number '
17. read num
18. write num ' is greater than 16'
19. write num ' is less than 16'
20. write num ' is equal to 16'.

Condition list continued

C6 num is numeric
C7 num > 16
C8 num < 16

For the diagram, see Fig. 5.4.

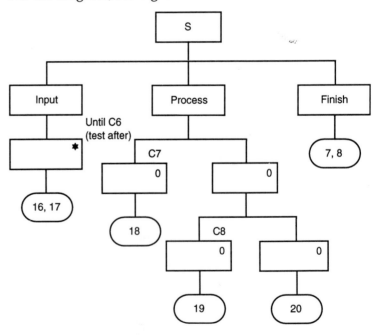

Figure 5.4

How an entry can be tested to see whether it is numeric or not is language-specific, so will not be dealt with here.

T

For '4. Tell you whether you are fat, thin or just right', the user will be asked for height (in centimetres) and weight (kilograms). The variables will be *Height* and *Weight*. *Weight* will be divided by *Height* to give *Factor*. If *Factor* is less than 0.34, the message will be 'thin'; if *Factor* is more than 0.49 the message will be 'fat'. Between, the message will be 'no problem'. (Please note that this formula has been invented just for this example and has no medical foundation whatever.)

As before, the input prompts will repeat until the input is numeric.

Action list continued

21. write prompt for height
22. read height
23. write prompt for weight
24. read weight
25. let factor = weight / height
26. write 'fat'
27. write 'thin'
28. write 'no problem'

Condition list continued

C9   Until height is numeric (test after)
C10 Until weight is numeric (test after)
C11 factor < 0.34
C12 factor > 0.49

For the diagram, see Fig. 5.5.

Subroutines

You will have noticed that the original problem has been solved by drawing not one, but five diagrams. The first was a simple diagram, on which the four boxes labelled H, D, S and T, and two others, were not refined. Simple convenience led to this, but it illustrates two important principles, **called top-down design** and **the use of subprograms or subroutines**. Top-down design is being used if the design of the solution *as a whole* is dealt with *first*, and the details are considered later. The initial diagram, which does not show detail, is called a **high level** diagram.

Later, the designs of the various parts of the program, as shown in the separate diagrams, can be developed separately. A block of code that is separated off from the rest is called a subroutine. When coding, the programmer should aim to make each subroutine as independent of the rest of the program as possible. The more independent each is, the

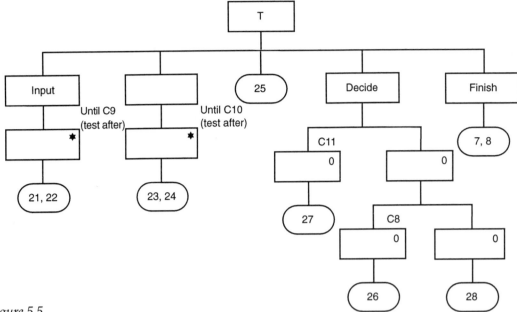

Figure 5.5

easier the program will be to read, the easier it will be to maintain, and the easier it will be to deal with errors and bugs. Subroutines usually take the form of **procedures** or **functions**, but making a distinction between the two would be beyond the scope of this book.

Repeated use of a subroutine

Each of the four diagrams above that deals with the choices on the menu ends with the sequence 7, 8. It is a small sequence, but it could be made into yet another subroutine, and, at the coding stage, coded only once. The same subroutine can be used, or 'called', many times in a program.

Nested menus

Users of packaged software will know that making a choice from a menu often causes another menu to appear. Making a choice from that may cause a third menu to appear, and so on. Often, in such cases, all the menus except the first one include the option of returning to the previous one. (Otherwise, pressing the escape key usually has that effect.) For an example let us suppose that if 'D' is chosen in the program above, the user is given a choice as to the nature of the message that will be displayed:

MESSAGE MENU
What sort of message would you like to leave?
1. A **Friendly** message
2. A **Loving** message

3. An **U**nfriendly message
4. A **S**exy message
5. **R**eturn to main menu
Key choice - F, L, U, S or R _.

If the user has made a choice in of F, L, U, S or R, a message of an appropriate nature will appear, and then the familiar 'Press Enter to return to the menu'. We must now decide which menu this means - the Main menu or the Message menu. It is likely in this case that the main menu should appear, but for completeness, both will be illustrated. A menu tree, similar to those found in manuals for packaged software, may help the explanations and this is shown in Fig. 5.6.

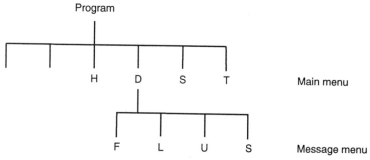

Figure 5.6

There are two possibilities. First, with direct return to the Main menu after successful display of the messages. Second, return to the Message menu after display of the messages.

First, Direct return to Main menu

Choosing D from the main menu gives the following design. For clarity only the second choice (L) is shown refined. The refinements of F, U and S would be similar.

New variable

Choice2   (Choice2 is a variable and so is all one word.)

Actions used before

8.   read k (and Enter)
11. write prompt for name-own
12. read name-own
13. write prompt for name-other
14. read name-other
15. write name-other, ', I love you - be mine for ever - ', name-own.

Actions continued

29. Write the message menu (writes several lines)

30. Write the message menu prompt,

'Key choice - F, L, U, S or R '

31. Read choice2
32. let choice2 = 'R'
33. write 'press Enter to return to *Main* menu

See Fig. 5.7.

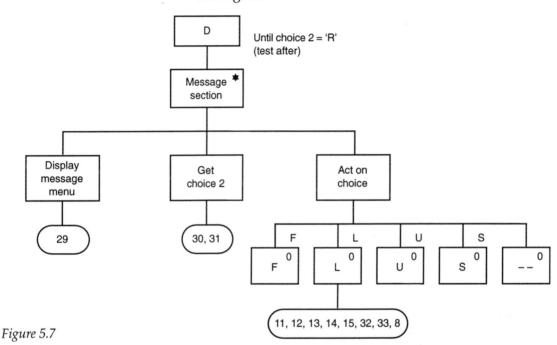

Figure 5.7

It has been assumed that the Loving message was the one used earlier, when there was no choice, and the refinement of L has been shown. When Enter is pressed, action 8, the condition on the repetition, is tested. Because of action 32, it is TRUE, so the box 'D' is complete.

Second, *with* return to the Message menu after successful display of the messages.
Choosing 'D' from the Main menu gives

New Actions

34. let choice2 = space
35. write 'press Enter to return to *Message* menu'.

The diagram is the same except that actions 34 and 35 replace actions 32 and 33. When Enter is pressed, action 8, the condition on the repetition, is tested. Because of action 34, it is FALSE, and

| Message section | is repeated.

Exercises 5

The programs to be designed in this set of exercises will be only skeletons that give you practice with handling menus but do not do anything useful. If the programs were to do something useful your time and attention would be diverted from dealing with the main point: the menus.

5.1 Design a program that presents the user with the menu

OPENING MENU
1. List the file
2. Modify entries in the file
3. Delete entries from the file
4. Add entries to the file
5. End the program

When any of 1–4 is selected, the program just prints a message showing which routine it went to, and then prompts the user with

Press 'M' for more or 'Q' to return to menu.

The response M should cause return to the same choice as before. Response Q should cause return to the opening menu.

When 5 is selected, the program terminates.

Error situations

(a) If, in the case of the opening menu, the user keys anything other than 1, 2, 3, 4 or 5, clear the screen and display the message

That was not a valid choice in range 1-5. Press Enter.

When Enter is pressed, the opening menu should be redisplayed.

(b) If, in the other case, the user keys anything other than R or Q, the opening menu should be displayed, just as if Q had been pressed.

5.2 Extend the design above so that if the user chooses '1. List the file', there is a new menu

THE LIST MENU
1. On Paper
2. On Screen
3. Return to opening menu

If 1 is chosen, show that the subroutine 'paper' was entered by displaying 'File is printing' five times. Likewise if 2 is chosen, show that the subroutine 'screen' was entered by displaying

'Screen output chosen' five times. After either of these, display the message 'Press Enter to continue' and when Enter is pressed, redisplay the LIST menu. If anything other than 1, 2 or 3 is keyed, redisplay the LIST menu.

5.3 Extend the design above so that if 2 is chosen, a third menu should be displayed

> THE SCREEN MENU
> 1. The first 20 records
> 2. The last 20 records
> 3. The whole file, a screen at a time
> 4. Every tenth record
> 5. Return to LIST menu

As before, if 1, 2, 3 or 4 is chosen, a message should be printed to stand for the routine that would be required in reality, followed by

> Press Enter to continue.

When Enter is pressed, the screen menu should be redisplayed.

6

Arrays

We are familiar with arrays in everyday life, although we may call them tables or lists (see Figs. 6.1–6.3).

Arrays (**tables** in COBOL), are very useful in programming, and simple ones are likely to be needed at quite an early stage. The simplest have only one dimension. The clearest word to use would be 'list', but list is a word with a special meaning in computing, so 'array' will have to do. An array is a set of variables (or records), all of the same data type, which are all given the same name. They are distinguished from one another by numbers called **subscripts**.

1	2	3	4	5
2	4	6	8	10
3	6	9	12	15
4	8	12	16	20
5	10	15	20	25

Figure 6.1 A familiar two-dimensional array: a multiplication table

	Weight in g not over	Rate pence
	60	25
Mon	100	38
Tue	150	47
Wed	200	57
Thu	250	67
Fri	300	77
Sat	350	88
Sun	400	100
	450	113

Figure 6.2 A simple one-dimensional array

Figure 6.3 First class postage rates: another familiar array

Figures 6.4 and 6.5 illustrate the differences between seven individual storage locations in memory, and a one-dimensional array with seven elements.

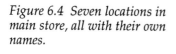

Figure 6.4 Seven locations in main store, all with their own names.

Size1   Size2   Size3   Size4   Size5   Size6   Size7

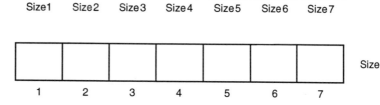

Figure 6.5 A seven-element (one-dimensional) array called Size

Size

1   2   3   4   5   6   7

To see the use of an array, consider the following example.

A shop sells greetings cards, and prices them by code. The codes are numbers 1 to 6. At one particular time, the prices are: for code 1, 35p; for code 2, 50p; for code 3, 65p; for code 4, 90p; for code 5, £1.20; and for code 6, £1.50. At some point in a program, the code is input, and the charge has to be displayed, according to the quantity of that code purchased. If an array were not used, the six prices would have to be separately named within the program, and a selection used:

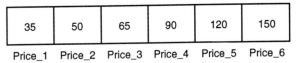

35	50	65	90	120	150

Price_1   Price_2   Price_3   Price_4   Price_5   Price_6

Condition list

C1 code = 1
C2 code = 2
C3 code = 3
C4 code = 4
C5 code = 5
C6 code = 6

Action list

1. let charge = price_1 * quantity
2. let charge = price_2 * quantity
3. let charge = price_3 * quantity
4. let charge = price_4 * quantity
5. let charge = price_5 * quantity
6. let charge = price_6 * quantity

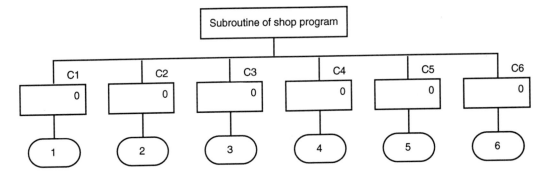

Figure 6.6

This is not difficult to code using CASE in Pascal or EVALU-ATE in COBOL, but if there had been 20 codes it would have been very clumsy and if there had been 100 it would have been dreadful. Of course, a shop would not sell cards at 100 different prices, but there are many businesses with a hundred codes for the things they deal in.

Using the concept of arrays, an array called *Price*, with 6 elements in it, would be declared, and the prices put in these elements.

35	50	65	90	120	150	All 6 loctions are called Price
1	2	3	4	5	6	

Thus *Price*[1] would contain 35, *Price*[2] would contain 50, and so on. The number in the brackets is the **subscript**. (Curved brackets are used in Basic and COBOL.) So, using an array, the whole of the design above would be reduced to this:

Action list

1. let charge = price[code] * quantity

The variable *Code* is used as the subscript, which is fine because *Code* is a positive integer. (An integer is a whole number.) There would be no conditions and no need for a selection. If there had been 100 codes, there would still have been only the one action.

To make the above example into a complete little program, we can suppose that the prices are written into the program, and that code and quantity are keyed in at the counter of the shop. The amount the customer should pay is displayed or printed. The program will need altering when the prices change. If code is –1, the program terminates. The program is used all day. Actions 2 to 7 are done only once, when the program is started.

Action list continued

2. let price[1] = 35
3. let price[2] = 50
4. let price[3] = 65
5. let price[4] = 90
6. let price[5] = 120
7. let price[6] = 150
8. write prompt for code and quantity
9. read code, quantity
10. write charge

Condition list

C1 code = –1

For the diagram, see Fig. 6.7.

You should now attempt exercises 6.1.

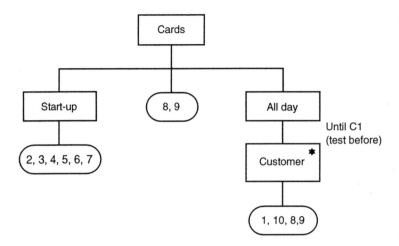

Figure 6.7

Storing data as it comes in

Leave the shop for a while, and look at a more abstract problem. Suppose a scientist wants to input up to 1000 readings
and then be told by his program what the middle reading
was. The readings are terminated by the rogue -1.

All that is needed is an array in which to store the readings and a variable to hold a subscript.

Variable list

reading	Numeric
read_array	Array of Numerics holding 1000
sub	Numeric, a subscript.

The subscript is initialized to 1. The first read is followed
by: Let read_array[sub] = reading. This causes the first reading to be stored in *Read_array*[1]. At the end, *Sub* is halved
to give the required answer, though this raises a slight complication there that has nothing to do with arrays.

Action list

1. let sub = 1
2. add 1 to sub
3. read reading
4. let read_array[sub] = reading
5. let sub = sub/2 [truncated]
6. write read-array[sub]

Condition list

C1 reading = –1

Note If there was an odd number of readings, the middle
one is wanted. For example, if there were seven readings,
the fourth is wanted: 1 2 3 $\underline{4}$ 5 6 7. If there was an even number
of readings, the one before the middle is wanted; e.g. if there
are eight, the fourth reading: 1 2 3 $\underline{4}$ 5 6 7 8. If there were
seven readings, *Sub* would be 8. 8/2 = 4, the number required.
If there were eight readings, *Sub* would be 9. 9/2 = 4.5. If

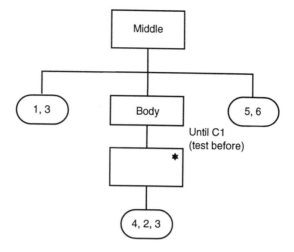

Figure 6.8

this answer is truncated we get 4, the number required. This is the reason why truncation is needed in action 5.

You should now attempt Exercise 6.2.

Searching an array

If in another program used by the card shop the question is, 'which code corresponds to a particular price that has been input?' there is again a saving if an array is used. Where there are only six codes this saving is not great, but where there are dozens, it is very significant. The technique is to use a repetition to inspect each element of the array in turn until the right one is found.

With the greetings cards example above, suppose the program 'needs to know' the code for a 65p card and that this is to be put in a variable called *Code*. The figure of 65p is in *Cost*. A third variable will be needed to act as a counter and a subscript. *Sub* would do as a name. *Sub* is given the value 1 at the start, and increased on each repeat, until either the required code is found or the whole array has been searched. Hence the following lists will be needed (NI is the variable's data type and means numeric integer):

Variable list	*Action list*
code NI	1. move 1 to sub
cost NI	2. add 1 to sub
sub NI	3. let code = sub
Price (an array of NI)	4. let code = 0

Condition list

C1 sub > 6
C2 price[sub] = cost

See Fig 6.9.

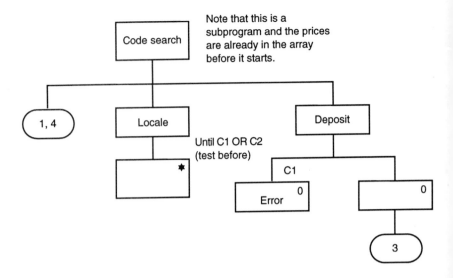

Fig 6.9

You are urged to follow Fig. 6.9 through until you are sure about how it works. With the given cost of 65, C2 will become true when *Sub* is 3, and Code_search will end with 3 in *Code*. If the cost had been 64, no match would have been found, Code_search would have ended with *Code* still containing 0, and *Sub* equal to 7. It is important to note that, on the repetition, C1 is tested before C2 because if C2 is attempted when sub is greater than 6, the program will terminate immediately with a message such as 'subscript out of range'. When coding it will be necessary to check that the language or compiler will handle a compound condition in such a way that if C1 is true, C2 will not be tested. If that is not the case, the design will have to be modified.

If there had been 100 codes instead of 6, C1 would have had to be 'sub > 100'. Nothing else would have had to be altered.

Adding one to a subscript is such a frequent action it is sometimes given the name **incrementing**. To increment a subscript is to add 1 to it. Similarly, to **decrement** a variable is to subtract 1 from it.

Self-checking numbers

As a further illustration of the usefulness of very simple arrays, so-called **self-checking numbers** will be considered. These numbers are commonly used for codes such as customer number, stock number and part number. If a mistake is made in copying such a number, including the copying involved when a number is entered at a keyboard, some arithmetic which the computer can do very quickly indeed will almost certainly pick up the error.

An extra digit is calculated and appended ('added') to

the number, on the right. The people using the numbers may well not be aware that the right-most digit is a **check digit**. A common system for calculating the extra digit is as follows.

Each digit is given a weighting: 2 for the units, 3 for the tens, 4 for the hundreds, etc. The digits are then multiplied by their weightings, and the sum of the products is divided by 11. If the remainder is neither 0 not 1, it is subtracted from 11 and the result is the check digit. If the remainder is 0, then 0 is used as the check digit. If the remainder is 1, subtraction from 11 would give 10. Because this is two digits it is ignored, and the number giving rise to it is not used. That probably sounds complicated. Three examples will show that it isn't really.

Example 1

Consider a four digit customer number, 1503.
Here is the number again, with the weightings above the digits:

    5432
    1503

Step 1. Multiply digits by weightings. $3 \times 2 = 6, 0 \times 3 = 0,$ $5 \times 4 = 20, 1 \times 5 = 5.$ (These are the products.)
Step 2. Add. $6 + 0 + 20 + 5 = 31$ (This is the sum of the products).
Step 3. Divide by 11: $31/11 = 2$ remainder 9
(Note that only whole numbers are used. 11 into 31 goes twice with 9 left over.)
Step 4. Subtract the remainder from 11. $11 - 9 = 2$

So, the check digit is 2, and the customer number becomes 15032.

Example 2

Consider a five digit stock number, 35426

Step 1. Multiply digits by weightings. $6 \times 2 = 12, 2 \times 3 = 6,$ $4 \times 4 = 16, 5 \times 5 = 25, 3 \times 6 = 18.$
Step 2. Add. $12 + 6 + 16 + 25 + 18 = 77$
Step 3. Divide by 11: $77/11 = 7$ remainder 0
Step 4. Not needed.

So, the check digit is 0, and the customer number becomes 354260

Example 3

Consider a four digit stock number, 4492

Step 1. Multiply digits by weightings. $2 \times 2 = 4$, $9 \times 3 = 27$, $4 \times 4 = 16$, $4 \times 5 = 20$.
Step 2. Add. $4 + 27 + 16 + 20 = 67$
Step 3. Divide by 11: $67/11 = 6$ remainder 1
Step 4. Not needed.

The number is unsuitable and will not be used.

The necessary steps will now be turned into a program design. A four digit number, like that used in examples 1 and 3, will be used.

The number will be put into an array called *Num-array*, with the thousands digit in position 1 and the units digit in position 4.

Using the first number considered above as an illustration we shall have:

Weighting	5	4	3	2	
	1	5	0	3	Num-array
Position	1	2	3	4	

The positions are almost the 'opposite' of the required weightings, so each digit will need to be multiplied by $(4 + 2 -$ position$)$. Check! You will see that $4 + 2 - 1 = 5$, $4 + 2 - 2 = 4$, $4 + 2 - 3 = 3$ and $4 + 2 - 4 = 1$. The position will be held in a variable called j. This will also control the repetition. Following the examples above, the result of step 1 will be placed in a variable called *Step1*, the result of step 2 into a variable called *Step2*, and so on. The check digit will be placed in *Chdig*. If the number is unsuitable, 'X' will be placed in a variable called *Flag*, which will otherwise contain spaces. The resulting lists are:

Variable list

num-array	(a 4–element array of NI)	
weighting	NI	
j	NI	
step1	NI	
step2	NI	*Condition list*
step3	NI	C1 $j > 4$
ch-dig	NI	C2 step3 $= 0$
flag	X	C3 step3 $= 1$

Action list

1. let weighting $= 4 + 2 - j$
2. let step2 $= 0$
3. let step2 $=$ step2 + Num-array[j] ∗ weighting
4. let step3 $=$ remainder from step2 / 11.

Note: C, Pascal and Cobol all have ways of obtaining a remainder easily, but they are all different.

5. let ch–dig = 0
6. let flag = ' '
7. let flag = 'X'
8. let step4 = 11 – step3
9. let j = 1
10. add 1 to j

Now the diagram can be drawn and is shown in Fig. 6.10.

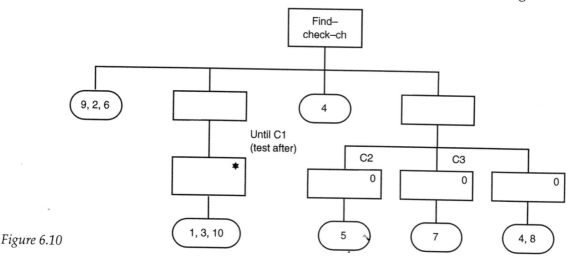

Figure 6.10

Flags

This example used a **flag**. Flags are common in programming. They are sometimes called switches. A flag is a variable used to show whether something has happened or not. Have you ever used one of those vacuum cleaners that has a 'bag-is-full' indicator? You don't have to open the machine and peer inside to see if the bag needs emptying. When it gets full, the indicator is set on. When you empty it, something sets the indicator off. Flags in programming are similar. If you use one, you must have: an action to set it on; an action to set it off; and a condition that tests it. In the subroutine above, there is no such condition because it is only a subroutine. The flag will be tested in the main program.

For

The type of repetition used above is very common when handling arrays. It is so common that programming languages have special words or **constructs** to handle it, and it is often called a **for** repeat. The setting of a **controlling variable** to an initial value, usually one, its increase at the end

> ### Reminder
>
> Since a flag only ever has two values there is a data type in some programming languages called **boolean**, especially useful for flags. A boolean variable can have only the values TRUE and FALSE. One bit in main store will be enough to hold it.

of each repeat, usually by one, and its testing against a limit, are all contained in one single instruction. It is useful, therefore, to have a way of showing a **for** in a design. In this book it will be done in the following way. The Condition list will be renamed the Condition and For list. Immediately after the condition that terminates the repetition will be a line giving the initial value and the increment size for the controlling variable. On the diagram, the * in the top right of the box will be accompanied by a + in the top left. FOR repetitions always have the test before, so it is not necessary to put that on the diagram. The design above would become:

Action list

1. let weighting = 4 + 2 − j
2. let step2 = 0
3. let step2 = step2 + Num-array[j] * weighting
4. let step3 = remainder from dividing step2 by 11.

Note: C, Pascal and Cobol all have ways of obtaining a remainder easily, but they are all different.

5. let ch-dig = 0
6. let flag   = ' '
7. let flag   = 'X'
8. let ch-dig = 11 − step3

Condition and For list

C1 j > 4
F1 j from 1 by 1
C2 step3 = 0
C3 step3 = 1

Now the diagram can be drawn (see Fig. 6.11).

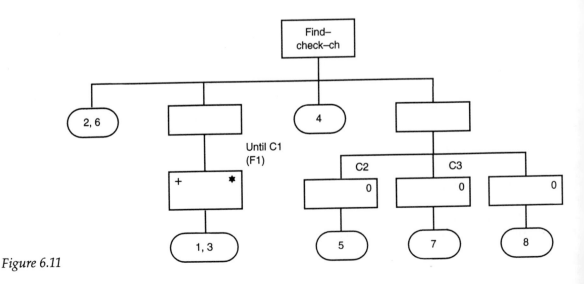

Figure 6.11

In design terms, the saving is minimal, but designers are usually coders too, and like to be able to show in the design exactly how the repeat will be controlled, in coding terms.

Decoding

Another use for arrays is the converting of codes into words that everyone can understand. The simplest of these occurs when the codes are whole numbers, starting near 1, and without big gaps. For example, suppose a small chain store has eight branches. For convenience these are given numbers. They are:

1. Lincoln	2 Grimsby
3. Boston	5. Worksop
6. Scunthorpe	7. Mansfield
8. Skegness	10. Newark

There used to be branches at East Retford and Doncaster, which were numbered 4 and 9, but these have been closed.

On all internal documents, the numbers are used for brevity, but on letters, statements, etc., to customers and suppliers, the full names need to be used. This is done by simply putting the eight names into the correct positions in a 10-element array, and using the reference number as a subscript. Positions 4 and 9 in the array would filled either with spaces or the word 'error'. A 15-element array would be better as it would allow for expansion in the future. Positions 11 to 15 would in the meantime be treated like positions 4 and 9.

Suppose that the full name is needed on an invoice, and that it would be written there from the variable O-branch-name. If the array were called Branch-name and the number of the branch were in the variable Branch-num, then the action

let o-branch-name = branch-name[branch-num]

would be all that was required.

The use of two matching arrays

Sometimes codes are not small numbers like those used above. Suppose that in the example, before computerization, the chain store had used three letters to denote a branch. The codes would then be

LIN, GRI, BOS, WOR, SCU, MAN, SKE and NEW.

These could be put in an array called, say, Branch-code. An array of branch names would also be declared, exactly as before.

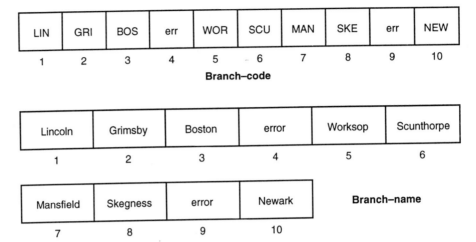

Figure 6.12

The two arrays would initially be filled with the necessary data so that they matched, as shown in Fig. 6.12.

Suppose that a code is read into a variable *I-branch-code*, and what is needed is the corresponding full name. The method is to search the array of codes until a match is found with the code in *I-branch-code*. The subscript that was pointing at the code is then used to pick up the full name. The design is therefore a modification of that used earlier to search an array. Before preparing it, it would be helpful to look again at the list of variables needed.

Input

i-branch-code

Output

o-branch-name

Working

branch-code   (a 10 element array)
branch-name   (a 10 element array)
sub   (a subscript and counter)

Action list

1. let o-branch-name = branch-name[sub]
2. let o-branch-name = 'error'

Condition and For list

C1 sub > 10
F1 sub from 1 by 1
C2 i-branch-code = branch-code[sub]

For the diagram, see Fig 6.13.

The repetition box may look rather odd, with no procedure or action attached to it. There is an action: the incrementing of sub. But this is incorporated into the For, so it does not show as a numbered action in a lozenge. It is important to note, as before, that on the repetition, C1 must be tested before C2, because if sub were greater than 10 and C2 were tested,

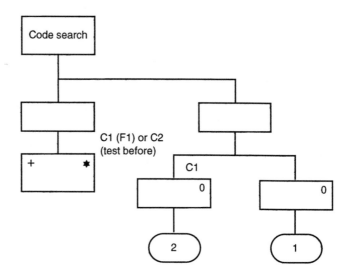

Figure 6.13

the program would be looking beyond the end of the array, and it would immediately terminate.

You should now attempt Exercises 6.3, 6.4 and 6.5.

Sorting into order

In Chapter 3 you were promised that a method of putting 10 words into alphabetical order, without drawing 3 000 000 boxes, would be found. There are many ways in which it can be done. They all use arrays. The one we shall look at is by no means the fastest, but it is fairly simple.

Let us suppose that we want to put several items in order, with the smallest first. It does not matter whether the items are words or numbers. The method is this. Put them into an array, in the order received. Go through the array, comparing pairs. Wherever a pair is in the wrong order, swap them over. So 1 and 2 are compared, then 2 and 3 are compared, then 3 and 4 are compared, and so on. Repeat this whole process and keep on repeating it until no swaps have to be made. Output the contents of the array.

For example, if we started with four numbers 56, 12, 23 and 15, and put them into a four element array, it would go like this:

```
 1    2    3    4
56,  12,  23,  15.    1 and 2 need swapping and we get
12,  56,  23,  15.    2 and 3 need swapping and we get
12,  23,  56,  15.    3 and 4 need swapping and we get
12,  23,  15,  56.
```

Start again. 2 and 3 need swapping and we get

```
12,  15,  23,  56.
```

Start again. Nothing needs swapping. Output results.

There are two repetitions:
(i) We go through the whole array, over and over again. That is the outer repeat and it goes on until all is in order.
(ii) We compare, and maybe swap, pairs, until the end of the data is reached.

(i) is the outer repetition, and (ii) is the inner repetition. Before (ii) starts, each time, a flag Swaps is set to false. Whenever a swap is needed, Swaps is set to true. Repetition (i) terminates when the flag Swaps shows that no swaps were done in a whole pass through the array by (ii).

A subscript will be needed. As it would be unusual to have an array just the right size, it will be assumed that we have to sort ten words and that the array will hold 18. A variable is needed to show how many words are being sorted so that we can restrict ourselves to inspecting only those elements that contain the data in which we are interested. We will not include here the method by which the data was loaded into the array. It could come from either a keyboard or, more likely, a file. For practice purposes it could be written into the program.

Variables

word	the 18-element array containing the 10 words in the first 10 elements, 1 to 10.
swaps	a **boolean** to control the outer repeat
j	subscript for the inner repeat.
max	the number of words being sorted.
temp	a store for one of the words being swapped over.

A **boolean** is a variable that can have only of two values, TRUE and FALSE

Before writing a formal action list, let us look further at what needs doing. When two items are swapped, a third, temporary, store is needed. Just to write

let a = b; let b = a

would result in both a and b containing what b contained originally.

Let temp = a; let a = b; let b = temp

achieves a swap. If instead of a and b we use adjacent elements in an array c, c[j] and c[j+1], then

let temp = c[j]; let c[j] = c[j+1]; let c[j+1] = temp achieves a swap. Now the action list can be written.

<table>
<tr><td>

Reminder

F stands for For. The number with F is the same as the number on the associated condition.

</td></tr>
</table>

Action list

1. let swaps = false
2. let swaps = true
3. let temp = word[j]
4. let word[j] = word[j+1]
5. let word[j+1] = temp
6. write word[j] to screen

Condition and For list

C1 swaps = false
C2 [j+1] > max
F2 j from 1 by 1
C3 word[j+1] < word[j]
C4 [j] > max
F4 j from 1 by 1

The comparison used in C2 involves [j+1] not j because C3 involves [j+1]. This is because each element in the array is compared with the one higher up, until there is no relevant data in the one higher up, or the end of the array is reached. For the diagram, see Fig. 6.14.

You should now attempt Exercises 6.6 and 6.7.

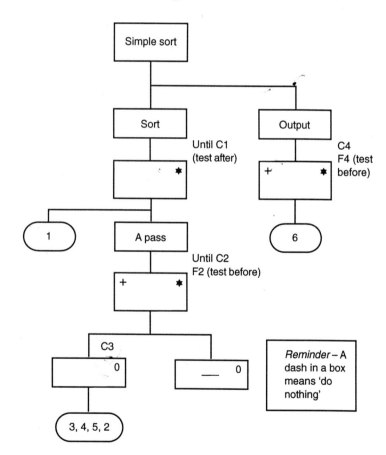

Figure 6.14 A program to put 10 words in alphabetical order without drawing 3 000 000 boxes.

Exercises 6

6.1 Prepare a design for a program to help a dentist prepare his/her bills. He/she does five kinds of work and the rates charged are:

1	Fillings	£14 per tooth
2	Extractions	£10 per tooth
3	Crowns	£50 per tooth
4	Dentures	£25 per tooth
5	Nerve-stripping	£20 per tooth

To the program are input patient-name, kind of work and number of teeth processed. He/she only ever does one kind of work in one session. The program prints a one line invoice. A patient-name of XXXX ends the program.

6.2 Design an averages program. It accepts the numbers, ended by –999 as a rogue. It then prints the mean (average) and also each number input. Beside each number is its difference from the mean (obtained by subtracting the mean from it). For example if the input were 25, 75, 50, –999, the output would be

```
Mean is 50
25     –25
75     +25
50      0              Allow for up to 200 numbers.
```

6.3 Design a routine to convert the numbers of the months into their names (e.g. 11 becomes November).

6.4 Design a routine so that days of the week, input as two letters, (Mo, Tu, We, Th, Fr, Sa, Su) are converted into the full names.

6.5* Design a program that will accept a weight in grams and print the first class postage charge, using the table at the beginning of the chapter. If the weight is over 450 grams, a message should be printed instead of a charge. *Hint*: use two matching arrays.

6.6 Design a routine to find the check digits for a selfchecking number that works as follows. The main number is six digits. To this two check digits are appended. The 'modulus', i.e. the number used for division, is 17. The weighting is 2, then 1, then 2, then 1, etc., starting from the right. For example, the working for 583614 is

$$4 \times 2 + 1 \times 1 + 6 \times 2 + 3 \times 1 + 8 \times 2 + 5 \times 1$$
$$= 8 + 1 + 12 + 3 + 16 + 5 = 45$$

$45/17 = 2$ remainder 11.
$17 - 11 = 06$. The number becomes 58361406.

6.7 Amend the design for a sort (see Fig. 6.14) so that it sorts into descending (instead of ascending) sequence.

7

File processing

For a computer, or any machine, to be able to process data, the data must have a **structure**. Many different structures are used: arrays, queues, stacks, **records, fields, files** and databases. Outside the central processing unit(CPU), the common arrangement is for characters to be grouped into fields, fields into records and records into files. A good example of a **file** is the phone book. In it, each entry is a **record**. For example,

Horne, P, 45 Grove St, Moldgreen HA5 6TY   Halifax 72965

would be a record. It is made up of four **fields**: name, address, exchange and number. The **characters** in the Exchange field are H,a,l,i,f,a and x.

Most computer processing depends on it being possible for the CPU to be able to retrieve data from one or more files, which are usually stored on magnetic disk or magnetic tape. Telecom has the phone books, in magnetic form, on their computers. When you ring Directory Enquiries, the clerk keys in the information on town, name and address, as you give it, and the computer program uses this to find the correct record in the file, which it displays on the clerk's screen. This is a example of **direct access**.

However, the handling of another kind of file, a **sequential file** or **serial file**, is easier for the beginner. With this sort of file, records can be retrieved, or read, only in the order in which they were written. The computer program has to start at the beginning and read every record until it gets to the one it wants. In quite a number of situations this is no disadvantage. A good example is a weekly or monthly payroll. All the employees will need to be paid, so every record in the file that keeps historical information such as pay-to-date and tax-paid-to-date, will need to be read. Starting at the beginning and dealing with each employee, one at a time, is as good a way as any of using the data on the file.

If a health centre wants to send letters to all male patients over 40 who haven't had their blood pressure checked in the last two years, the program will have to inspect every patient record in turn to see if all the criteria are met.

Reading a file

As files are usually made up of records, one *read*, when it refers to a file, usually retrieves one record. That is what will be assumed in this chapter. Files usually contain hundreds of records - maybe tens of thousands. The read that retrieves one must therefore be inside a repetition. Files normally vary in length as they are used. Health centres lose patients and gain new ones. Employees leave or retire; new ones join the organisation. Hence, at the time of writing the program, it will not be known exactly how many records there will be to read. It it therefore necessary to be able to detect the end of the file in some way so that the repeated reading can stop. A simple method is to have a dummy record at the end of the file, like the **dummy data** used in chapter 3. This record has the same format as the others but is not processed. For example, if the health centre uses surname as the main way of identifying clients, and keeps the client file in alphabetical order of surname, the **dummy record** may have Zzzz as surname.

To illustrate very simple file processing we will suppose that the health centre is moving to new premises and the staff decide to send a letter to every client, telling them about this. They want to use the computer to print the name and address labels, one for each client. (In reality it is hoped that they would need only one for each address, but that would be too complicated for us just now.)

It might seem at first glance that the design would be

Variable list

Input (in-record)	*Output* (out-record)
i-name	o-name
i-address	o-address
i-other-data	

It is worth noting here that the records in the client file will contain many fields besides the three listed above. That does not matter. The program will have to receive all the data and find room for it in main memory, but it does not have to use it all. In the design we need refer only to data that we need for the application with which we are dealing.

Action list

1. read in-record into i-name, i-address, i-other data
2. let o-name = i-name

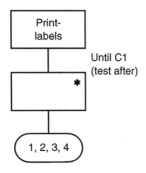

Figure 7.1 Note that this is not a good design

3.   let o-address = i-address
4.   write out-record

Condition list

C1 i-name = 'Zzzz'

Reading ahead

A problem with this program is that it will print a label addressed to Zzzz. At worst this will result in a puzzled postman and the waste of a label and postage stamp. However, in a more normal program the results would be more serious. If there was arithmetic to be done, some strange results would be be produced, or, if the input record did not contain numeric data in the right places, the program might stop abnormally. Worse, a record containing rubbish might get written to a master file. If the file were empty (a file can be empty), the let instructions would have no data to act upon. This again might cause abnormal termination. All these problems can easily be avoided by having one read before the repetition is entered and then having the main read within the repeat as the last action in the sequence. The 'Second proper adding program' in Chapter 3 worked like that.

Opening and closing

Another shortcoming of the design is that the files have been neither opened nor closed. What actually happens when a computer file is open and closed is beyond the scope of this book. It is enough to say that opening and closing are necessary and ought to be in the design. A much better design would therefore be:

Action list

1.   read in-record into i-name,
     i-address, i-other data
2.   let o-name = i-name
3.   let o-address = i-address
4.   write out-record
5.   open client-file
6.   close client-file

Condition list

C1 i-name = 'Zzzz'

See Fig 7.2.

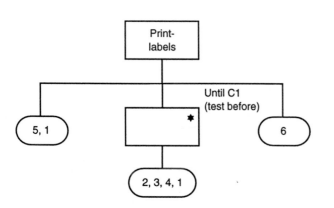

Figure 7.2

Now, as soon as the dummy record is read, C1 will become true and the repetition will end, so that actions 2,3 and 4 will not be applied to the dummy data. If the file is empty, the repetition will never start.

All simple programs reading just one serial file will have the same form as the one above. Only the processing will change. There may be some actions before the repeat, in addition to open and first read. There may be some actions after the repeat in addition to the close. The main processing, represented by actions 2, 3 and 4 above, will change, of course.

Example

As a result of a traffic census, a file called census-file was created, with one record for each vehicle. Among the fields in each record were vehicle-type and number of passengers carried. The vehicle-types were 1 for a car, 2 for a bus or coach and 3 for any other vehicle. The end of the file was marked by a record with 9 in vehicle-type. The output required was: the percentage of passengers that travelled by car, and the percentage of passenger-carrying vehicles that were cars. (All the occupants of cars were assumed to be passengers. Vehicle-type 3 vehicles were assumed to be carrying no passengers).

Variable lists

Input
All input fields are part of a record called in-rec

i-type	C	vehicle-type
i-no-pass	NI	Number of passengers

Output
Record name out-rec

o-pc-pass-car	ND	Car passengers as a percentage of all passengers
o-pc-car	ND	Cars as a percentage of all vehicles

Calculations
o-pc-pass-car will be (total number of passengers in type 1 vehicles)/(total number of passengers) * 100.

o-pc-car will be (total number of type 1 vehicles)/(total number of type 1 vehicles + total number of type 2 vehicles) * 100.

For these calculations to be possible, more variables will be needed. As these do not appear in either the input or the output, they will be called work variables:

Work variables

w-1-count   counts type '1' vehicles
w-2-count   counts type '2' vehicles
w-car-pass   counts passengers in type '1' vehicles
w-total-pass counts passengers in any type of vehicle

Each of the work fields will need to be initialized to zero, and each will need to have something added to it.

Action list

1. open files
2. close files
3. read record from census-file

(This reads data into all input variables in one go)

4. write o-pc-pass-car
5. write o-pc-car
6. let w-1-count, w-2-count, w-car-pass, w-total-pass = 0
7. add 1 to w-1-count
8. add 1 to w-2-count
9. add i-no-pass to w-car-pass
10. add i-no-pass to w-total-pass
11. let o-pc-pass-car = w-car-pass/w-total-pass * 100
12. let o-pc-car = w-1-count/(w-1-count + w-2-count) * 100

Condition list

C1 i-type = '1'
C2 i-type = '2'
C3 i-type = '9'

For the diagram, see Fig. 7.3.

   As is often the case, there are other possible designs. It is important to note that the percentages cannot be calculated until after all the records have been read, that is, after the repetition is over. Therefore, in this case, there is no Write inside the repeat. The read ahead and read next boxes were not essential but were inserted above action 3 to emphasise it.

   You should now attempt Exercise 7.1 at the end of the chapter.

System detection of end of file

There is a neater way of detecting the end of a file than the use of a dummy record. In Basic, Pascal and C there is a function EOF, and in Cobol a condition called END. When the operating system detects the end of the file it signals this to (the machine code version of) your program by setting EOF or END to TRUE. Unfortunately, however, in some cases (Pascal and most Basics) the end of the file is detected at the time the last record is read, whilst in other cases (e.g.

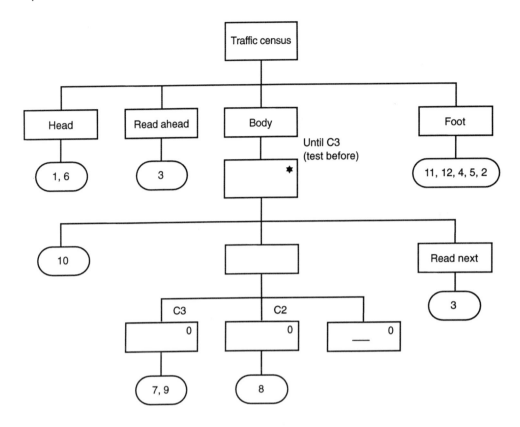

Figure 7.3

Cobol), it is detected only when the read fails because there is no record to be read.

The second of the two ways fits very well with the design used when a dummy record ended the file. The only change necessary in the example is to C3, which becomes: C3 end-of-census-file. The format of that special condition is end-of-<filename>. This works, of course, only if there is no dummy record.

In the first of the two ways, where the program 'knows' it has the last record as soon as it has received it, everything would be equally simple if it were not for the fact that with most operating systems it is possible to have an empty file, that is, a file containing no data. Due to this fact, there is a problem with distinguishing an empty file from one that contains just one single record. Consider the partial designs shown in Figs. 7.4 and 7.5.

The design in Fig. 7.4 would work in all cases except where the file contained no data. If there were no data, the procedure Process would have nothing to work on.

The design in Fig. 7.5 works if the file is empty, and goes on working until the end of the file is reached, but the last record does not get processed.

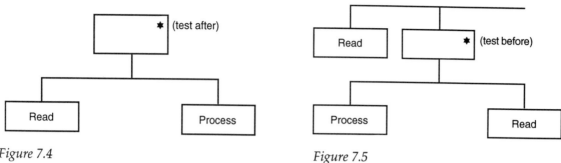

Figure 7.4   Figure 7.5

There is no simple solution. The best that can be done is probably to use the first of the two methods above, but test the file first to see if it is empty or not and not even proceed to the logic shown, if it is indeed empty.

Loading arrays from files

It is often the case that for a program to handle data it should be in an array (table) in main memory. However, it is seldom a good idea to store the data in the program, because that means that every time the data changes, the program has to be changed. That means that it has to be recompiled, and retested, because any change to a program, however slight, can introduce a error. In the chapter on arrays, one example used was a small chain store with a dozen branches. In such a business it is probable that branch numbers would be related to names in many programs. If the names were coded into the programs, then every time a branch was opened or closed, dozens of programs would have to be recompiled and retested. When data changes often, as in the cases of prices in a shop, coding the data into the program would be totally impractical.

It is normal practice, therefore, to hold data in a file on backing store, and for a program that needs to reference it frequently to start its execution by opening the file, reading the contents into an array in main store and then closing the file (so that other programs running concurrently can also use it). To see how this affects design, the greetings cards problem from Chapter 6 on arrays will be looked at again. It was as follows.

A shop sells greetings cards, and prices them by code. The codes are numbers 1 to 6. At one particular time, the prices are: for code 1, 35p; for code 2, 50p; for code 3, 65p; for code 4, 90p; for code 5; £1.20 and for code 6, £1.50. At some point in a program, the code is input, and the charge has to be displayed, according to the quantity of that code purchased.

It was assumed that the prices were already in the array when the following design was given.

Action list

1.   let charge = price[1] * quantity

Let us suppose now that the prices are in a file called *Prices file*. Each record has two fields:

> i-code
> i-price, in pence.

There is no dummy record at the end. It will be assumed that the file always contains at least one record, and that the programming language used will detect EOF when the last record is read. It will also be assumed, for now, that the file never contains more than 10 records, for 10 codes. A code might no longer exist. If so, it will not be on the file. As we cannot have elements in the array which are empty, all of them will be initialized to 999. Where a code exists, this figure will be overwritten.

   The initialization will need a FOR repetition. The reading of the file can be controlled by testing EOF, after each repeat.

Working fields

w-price   an array of integers
w-sub   a subscript

Action list

1.   let w-price[i-code] = i-price
2.   let w-price[w-sub] = 999
3.   let w-sub = 1
4.   add 1 to w-sub
5.   open prices-file
6.   read prices-file record into i-code, i-price
7.   close prices-file

Condition list

C1 w-sub > 10
      F1 w-sub from 1 by 1
C2 end-of-prices-file

For the diagram, see Fig. 7.6.

   This design was based on one rather rash assumption: that the file would never contain more than 10 records. The snag is that if it contained more, the program would **terminate abnormally** because the subscript *W-sub* would go **out of range**. That is, on reaching 11 *W-sub* would be used to access the non-existent eleventh element of the array, *W-price*. Abnormal terminations are always best avoided. Even

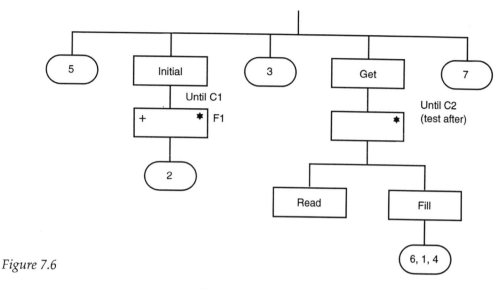

Figure 7.6

if it is not sensible for the program to continue, because an unexpected situation has occurred, the program should issue a meaningful message, and close files, before stopping. The improvements can be incorporated with a small modification, requiring one extra action.

Action

8. write 'file has more than 10 prices and array is full' to screen

The condition on the second repeat needs altering too. The diagram becomes as shown in Fig. 7.7.

General guidelines

Up to this point, solutions to problems given as examples have been developed without, apparently, following any plan. This is partly because the programs have been very small, and partly because the emphasis has been on the different little sub-problems that the programmer is liable to come across. It is time for a set of general guidelines which can be followed in most cases. One thing that makes computer programming so interesting is that every problem is different. For that reason, these are guidelines not rigid rules. It will not always be sensible to follow them completely. That is not, however, an invitation to skip as many steps as possible and revert to just getting on with the coding! You should follow them as far as you can if you want to minimise the frustrations of debugging and produce a maintainable program.

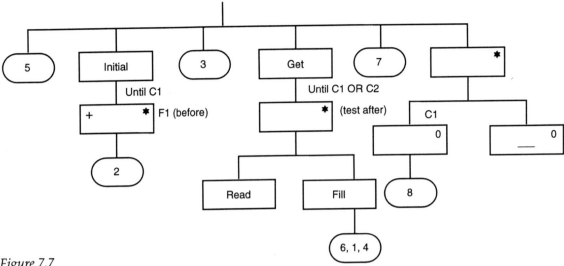

Figure 7.7

The steps in program design

1. Compose a *small* amount of input data.
2. Work out, and write down, the expected outcomes.
3. Make a note of the steps taken in working out the results. The purpose of these first three steps is to make sure that you fully understand the nature of the input and output data, and the processing necessary to get from one to the other.
4. Make lists of variables as far as possible.
5. Write down, maybe informally, the main repetitions and their controlling conditions.*
6. Write down, maybe informally, the main activities.*
7. Formalize the conditions.*
8. Write an action list.*
9. Draw a first attempt at a diagram.
10. Allocate the actions and conditions to the diagram.
11. Improve the diagram.
12. Dry run the design.
13. Alter the three lists and the diagram as necessary.
14. Repeat steps 12 and 13 until the design is satisfactory.

* Add to the variable lists as necessary.

You should now attempt Exercise 7.2 at the end of the chapter.

Control breaks

To understand what this jargon phrase means, a few other things need explaining first. Serial files that are not merely temporary are nearly always in sequence, and are therefore **sequential** files. A familiar non-computer file is the phone book. That is sequential. It is in sequence by surname, and within that by initial. Because these fields surname and initial are the ones we use to help us find the record we want, they are call **key fields**. Telecom probably keeps a file of its subscribers in sequence by telephone number, and that field is therefore the key field. A school may keep a list of its pupils in sequence by class or form, and within that by surname, so form and surname are the key fields. It is often the case with such files that there is more than one **key**.

A change of data in a key field is called a **control break**.

It is often the case that when a sequential file is printed or examined, totalling is required, and to have a total every time a key field changes. Taking the school example, it would be useful to have the computer printing the total number of pupils in each form. These totals would be triggered by the control break which occurred when the field *form* changed.

It is useful to look at the design of such a program because it illustrates very nicely the connection between the structure of data and the structure of the program that reads or writes it.

Example

The Tick-Tock clock company keeps an order file. The fields on the file are:

Order number
Date of order
Customer number
Delivery date
Model
Quantity

The company makes 10 or 12 different kinds of clock, shown by a code in the Model field. The file is kept in delivery date sequence, but within each date the orders are in sequence by model. If a customer wants clocks of more than one model, separate orders are filed. The company makes large quantities, and there will be several orders for each model for each delivery date.

A program is required that prints out a list showing how many clocks of each model are required on each day in the future. The program must read through the file, and must list each model and give the total required. Each page must be given a heading which starts with the date. There must be a total for all models for each date, There must also be a grand total of all clocks on order. The printout must start with a title page. The list for each day is to start on a new page. The grand total is to be on a separate page, at the end. So that delivery dates can be compared easily, they are stored in the form yyddd, where ddd is the day of the year. For example 14 Feb 1995 is stored as 95045 because 14 February is the 45th day of the year.

If, in an extremely slack period, the only orders for delivery on 95045 were as shown in the Table, the page in the printout for that date would be as shown in Fig. 7.8.

Orders for delivery

Order no	Date of order	Customer no	Delivery date	Model	Quantity
1235	94123	3467	95045	4	25
1463	94222	2365	95045	4	35
1753	95003	1124	95045	8	10
4730	94333	2313	95045	8	90
3124	95010	3467	95045	8	75

In practice the date would be converted to something readable before printing, but this example is not about date conversion.

Once we are certain about how the output above was obtained from the input, we can continue the design process by looking at the structure of the *output data*. First, this consists of page after page after page: that is, a repeat of page, preceded by a title page and followed by the grand total. Each main page consists of three parts: the headings (lines 1–4 below), the body of the page (lines 5 and 6 below), and the totals for the day (lines 7–9 below). The body of a page is a repeat of the totals for each model.

This structure can be represented in the form of a diagram very similar to that which has been used for programs (see Fig 7.9).

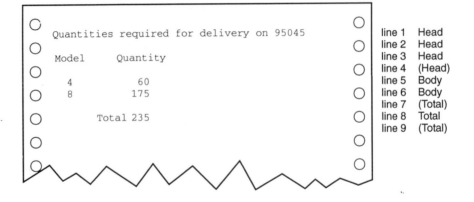

```
Quantities required for delivery on 95045          line 1   Head
                                                   line 2   Head
   Model        Quantity                           line 3   Head
                                                   line 4   (Head)
      4             60                              line 5   Body
      8            175                              line 6   Body
                                                   line 7   (Total)
          Total 235                                line 8   Total
                                                   line 9   (Total)
```

Figure 7.8

The next step in the design process is to look at the structure of the *input data*. First, it consists of groups of records with the same date: there is a repetition of date groups. Each date group consists of model groups: within each date group is a repetition of model group. Finally, each model group consists of several records: within each model group there is a repetition of record.

This structure also can be represented in the form of a diagram (Fig. 7.10) very similar to that which has been used for programs.

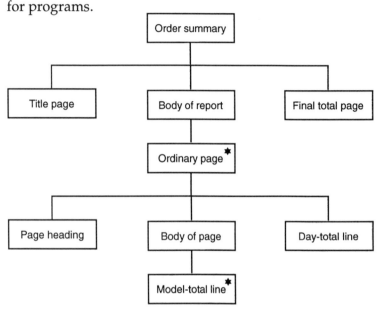

Figure 7.9 The structure of the output data

The program structure will be created by combining Figs. 7.9 and 7.10 and then allocating the actions and conditions. But first it is necessary, as usual, to list the input, output and working variables.

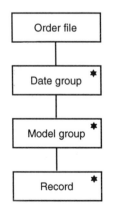

Figure 7.10 The structure of the input data

Input variables

order-no
date-of-order
customer-no
deliv-date
model
quant

Output variables

title-page	(a literal)
page-heading	(a literal with deliv-date)
column-headings	(some literals)
model-total-line	(model and model-total)
day-total-line	(day-tot)
final-total-page	(grand-tot)

Working variables

w-deliv-date
w-model

The reason for the working variables is that is it necessary to be able to tell when the model and delivery date change so that the printing of the model total lines and the page changes can be triggered.

The actions and conditions should be self-explanatory, except that it must be noted that end of file must be tested for on all repetitions, and, when using a system or language that detects end of file only when an attempt to read fails, the test for end of file must come first.

Action list

1. let w-deliv-date = deliv-date
2. let w-model = model
3. let model-total = 0
4. let day-tot = 0
5. let grand-tot = 0
6. add quant to model-total, date-total, grand-total
7. open order file
8. read record from order file
9. write title page
10. write page-heading
11. write model-total-line
12. write day-total-line
13. write final-total-page
14. close order file

Condition list

C1 end-of-file
C2 deliv-date > w-deliv-date
C3 model not = w-model

The diagram will, as predicted earlier, be a slight adaptation of the two data structures. Before any iterations at all, we can print the title page, open the input file, read the first record and zero the grand total. So actions 9,7,5 and 8 go on the diagram at the start. The printing of the grand total and the closing of the file, actions 13 and 14, go right at the end, after all iterations have finished.

Before the body of a page is printed, the page heading needs writing. This is also the place to zero the date-total, and to store the new delivery date. These are actions 10, 4 and 1. If action 1 is not done here, we shall not get into the next iteration. At the end of each page comes the date total, action 12.

Each line in the body of the page is a model-total. One of these totals is printed each time *model* changes, that is, each time we come out of the lowest iteration. So action 11 goes on the diagram to the right of the lowest iteration. Before this lowest-level iteration, the model total needs zeroing, and the new *model* needs storing so actions 2 and 3 go there.

At the lowest level, each record is processed, and then the attempt is made to read the next record. Processing consists merely of adding the quantity into the three total fields. So actions 6 and 8 go at the lowest level. That disposes of all the actions and the design is complete(Fig. 7.11).

You should now attempt Exercises 7.3 and 7.4. Able students should also attempt Exercise 7.5.

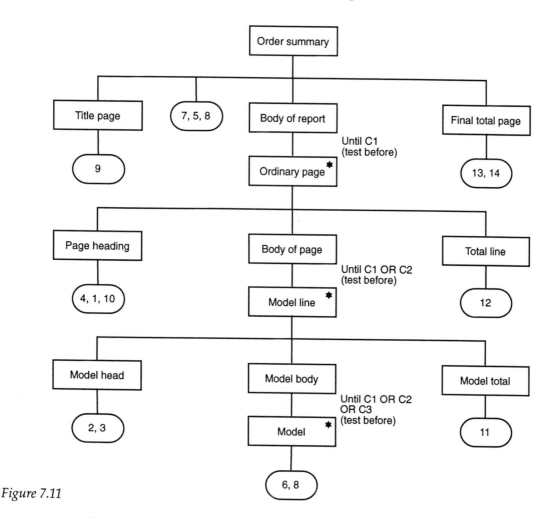

Figure 7.11

Exercises 7

7.1 Prepare a design for the following problem. A company that makes springs keeps records of its sales on a file called 'sales'. Three of the fields are: customer type, quantity sold, and item price. Customer type is either 'S' (special) or 'O' (ordinary).

The program is to print a line, for each record input, showing all these fields and in addition the gross cost (obtained by multiplying quantity sold by item price) and amount due. The amount due will be the gross cost less, possibly, one or two discounts. If gross cost is greater than £150, there will be a discount of 10%. If the customer type is 'S' there will be a discount of £2. A customer may receive both discounts. In addition to the above, the program should print a figure showing how many customers received the 10% discount.

You should produce: very small amount of sample data; the results expected from this; Lists of variable names for input, output and work fields; Action and condition lists, and a structure diagram.

Note that the words/terms: variable, data name, identifier, variable name, data-item and field have very similar meanings, and may be taken as all meaning the same thing in this context.

7.2* Prepare a design for the following problem. A club that encourages family membership keeps records of its members on a file called 'members'. Six of the fields are: member surname, member address, number of adults in family, number of older children in family, number of young children in family and a flag showing whether their subscription is due or not paid (P = paid, U = unpaid). The program is to print, for each family with subscription unpaid, a line showing all these fields and in addition the amount due. This will be calculated as follows: £3 for each adult, £2 for each older child and £1 for each young child. However, the maximum for any family is £10. In addition to the above, the program should print a figure showing how many families are owing money and the total amount due from all the families.

You should produce: a very small amount of sample data; the results expected from this; lists of variable names for input, output and work fields; action and condition lists, and a structure diagram.

7.3 Improve the decoding example in Chapter 6 so that the names of the shops in the chain are held on a little file that is read into an array each time the program is started. The situation was this.

A small chain store has eight branches. For convenience these are given numbers. They are:

1. Lincoln   2. Grimsby
3. Boston   5. Worksop

6. Scunthorpe   7. Mansfield
8. Skegness   10. Newark

There used to be branches at East Retford and Doncaster, which were numbered 4 and 9, but these have been closed.

On all internal documents, the numbers are used for brevity, but on letters, statements, etc., to customers and suppliers, the full names need to be used.

Design a program that will load the names from the file, accept a number from the keyboard and display the name of the corresponding branch. It should repeatedly accept numbers from the keyboard until branch 99 is keyed.

7.4* Telecom print itemised bills for customers who request them, where the call costs more than 50p. Your exchange, which is now a computer, writes a record for every such call. The record has six fields:

Number calling
Exchage called (STD code)
Number called (extra to the STD code)
Number of units used
Date
Time

On the bill is printed, amongst other things, the name of the exchange called. Design two subroutines for the billing program. The first should open a file of exchange names, with their STD codes, and read all these names and numbers into a paid of matching arrays and then close the file. The second should, on being given an STD code, provide the corresponding exchange name.

Here are some example records from the file of exchanges:

0203	COVENTRY
0204	BOLTON
0205	BOSTON
0206	COLCHESTER
0207	DERWENTSIDE
0208	BODMIN
021	BIRMINGHAM
0222	CARDIFF

7.5 Adapt the control break program given in the chapter (see Fig. 7.11), as follows. Two dates are prompted for and keyed in, and it lists order totals between those two dates only.

7.6 A university faculty of science runs many courses. Details about applicants for the courses are kept on file. Each record shows, among others, the following fields:

Student name
Offer code; D = definite, P = provisional, X = not yet.

Course name
Points

The records are firstly in alphabetical order by course, from Astronomy and Botany through to Zoology. Within that they are in order by Offer Code. (Within that they are in alphabetical order by name, but that does not affect the design.) The field called Points relates to 'A' level grades. A is rated 5, B is rated 4, C is rated 3 and so on, so two Bs and one C would come to 11.

A design is required for a program that will list all applicants. Each course is to start on a new page. Every time Offer Code changes, the average points per applicant in the group is to be printed, and also the number of applicants in the group. These two figures are also to be given for each course. The first group will be those applicants for astronomy who have been given definite offers.

7.7* An estate agent keeps details of all property for sale on a sequential file that is in sequence by asking price. The asking price is the advertised price. A program runs once a week giving summary information. It creates seven price bands and for each band it gives:

the number of properties in the band
the potential total commission from all the properties in the band.

At the end, it gives:

the total number of properties on the file
the total potential commission from all the properties.

On average, a property sells for 94% of the asking price, and the commission charged is 1.25%. Hence the potential commission for a property is

asking price * 0.94 * 0.0125.

The bands are: up to £40000
£40001 to £55000   £80001 to £100000
£55001 to £65000   £100001 to £125000
£65001 to £80000   £125001 and above.

Design a program to provide the information required. It should follow the control break logic shown in the chapter.

8

Validation

Raw input cannot be trusted. There is always a chance that it is faulty in some way. The famous acronym GIGO, meaning garbage in, garbage out, neatly summarizes the fact that the output from a program can be correct only if the input was correct. To be added to that is the fact that if a field that is supposed to contain a number actually contains something else, the program will fail; in the formal jargon we say, 'terminate abnormally', and in the slang we say, '**crash**'.

Most input nowadays is validated field by field as it is keyed. It is that kind of validation that will be dealt with in this chapter.

The two ways in which programs in different languages differ most from each other are the ways in which output is formatted, and the ways in which the details of validation are done. Therefore, in this chapter, some of the details will have to be left out. Where this is done, it will, as far as possible, be pointed out.

Checking that a value is numeric

The golden rule is that raw data should not be accepted into a variable of numeric type. It should be accepted only into one of non-numeric type. This may be an array of characters (standard Pascal), a string (extended Pascal and Basic), or an alphanumeric item (Cobol). C is more flexible.

The characters entered should be checked to see if they are numeric. If they are, they should be transferred to a numeric field, with type conversion as necessary. If they are not, the user should be reprompted, perhaps with a helpful message.

A number may, of course be negative, and the sign may be entered in more than one way. Also, a number may contain a decimal point. *To begin with, only positive integers (that is, unsigned whole numbers) will be considered.*

An outline solution, using no change of prompt, would be as shown in Fig. 8.1.

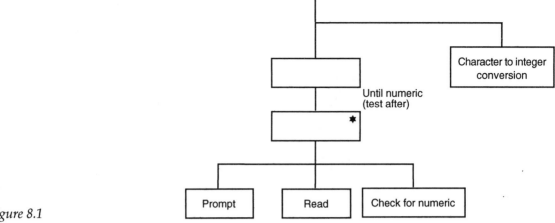

Figure 8.1

If a message or change of prompt is required when the user makes a mistake, the outline would become as shown in Fig. 8.2.

There must be some limit to the size of number. Eight digits have been chosen here.

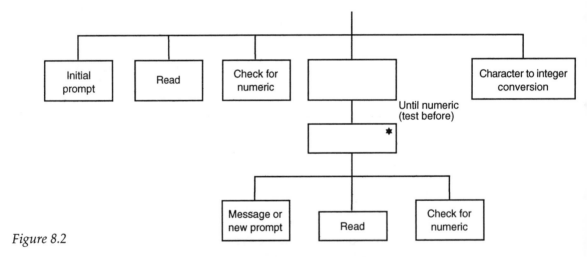

Figure 8.2

It will be assumed that the Read procedure starts by initial-izing an array of characters, called *In-arr,* to spaces, as shown in the left half of Fig. 8.3. It will then cause the input, lim-ited to eight digits, to be keyed into this array. If a four digit number 5638, is keyed in, *In-arr* will then be as shown in the left half of Fig. 8.4.

The procedure 'Check for numeric' will check that *In-arr* contains only digits and spaces, with all the digits at the beginning of the array and all the spaces at the end. This means that *In-arr*[1] will contain a digit. All the other ele-ments may contain spaces. The details of this procedure will have to be **language-specific**, so will not be covered here.

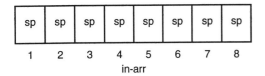 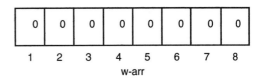

Figure 8.3

The task of the procedure 'Character to integer conversion' is to get the separate digits, which are characters in *In-arr*, into the form of a number, in a numeric variable. The general strategy will be to get the digits into an array of integers and then assemble these separate digits into a number. Using our example, that means first changing '5', '6', '3', '8' into 5, 6, 3, 8 and then into 5638.

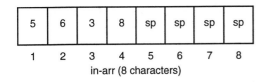 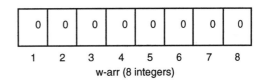

Figure 8.4

Besides the array of integers and the final numeric item, four other variables will be needed. The complete variable list will be as follows:

Input

in-arr   an array of characters from 1 to 8

Work

w-arr   an array of integers from 1 to 8
sub   a subscript
top   an integer showing the length of the number
power   a power of 10. The need for this will be seen later

Output

o-number   an integer

The array of integers, *W-arr*, will be initialized to all zeros as in the right half of Fig. 8.3. Next it will be necessary to find out how many digits there are in *In-arr*. A repetition will be needed that both counts the digits and stops when a space is reached. The result of this counting will be stored in *Top*. The first digit then needs transferring to the first position in *W-arr*, the second needs transferring to *W-arr*[2] and so on until all the digits (but none of the spaces), have been transferred. Using our example of 5638, *Top* will contain 4 and when the transfer is complete the arrays will be as shown in Fig. 8.5.

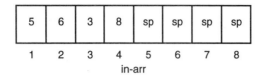
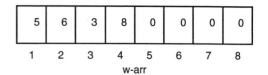

Figure 8.5

The next stage will be to multiply the tens digit by 10, the hundreds digit by 100 and so on. If you study Fig. 8.6 and think about it, you will see that this means multiplying *W-arr*[1] by 10 to the power of (*Top-1*), *W-arr*[2] by 10 to the power of (*Top-2*) and so on.

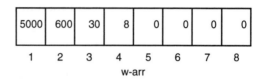

Figure 8.6

The final stage will be to add the numbers in W-arr together and put the sum in 0-number. Using our example, this will be 5000 + 600 + 30 + 5, or

let o-number = w-arr[1] + w-arr[2] + w-arr[3] + w-arr[4]

These plans result in the design that follows: The various parts are explained below the diagram, Fig. 8.7.

Action list

1. let in-arr[sub] = space
2. let w-arr[sub] = 0
3. let top = 8
4. let top = sub - 1
5. let w-arr[sub] = in-arr[sub]
6. let power = top - sub
7. let w-arr[sub] = w-arr[sub] * 10^{power}
8. let 0-number = 0
9. add w-arr[sub] to o-number

Note that action 5 involves a change of type so that in Pascal and Basic a function will have to be used in place of a simple assignment.

Condition list

C1 (until) sub > top
  F1 from 1 by 1
C2 (until) sub > top OR in-arr[sub] = space
  F2 sub from 1 by 1
C3 (until) sub > top
  F3 sub from 1 by 1

For the diagram, see Fig. 8.7

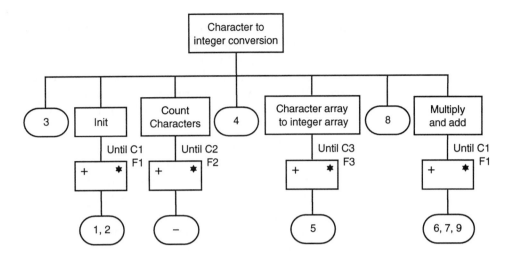

Figure 8.7

Action 3 initializes *Top* to the size of the two arrays. 'Init' initializes *In-arr* to all spaces and *W-arr* to all zeros.

'Count chars' counts the digits. In our example, when sub reaches 5, In-arr[sub] will be a space. This will make C2 true and the repetition will stop. Action 4 will then assign to Top the actual number of digits. In our example, *Top* will become $5 - 1 = 4$.

'Character array to integer array' will transfer the digits from *In-arr* to *W-arr*. The repeat is limited by the new value in Top.

'Multiply and add' multiplies each digit by the right power of 10 and adds the result to *0-number*. Using our example, the steps are:

the for mecahnism sets *Sub* to 1

Action 6 makes *Power* = $4 - 1 = 3$

Action 7 replaces the 5 in *W-arr*[1] by $5*10^3$ (i.e. 5000)

Action 9 adds the 5000 to *0-number*

The for mechanism increments *Sub* to 2

Action 6 makes *Power* = $4 - 2 = 2$

Action 7 replaces the 6 in *W-arr*[2] by $6*10^2$ (i.e. 600) and so on.

Being more user friendly

A user inputting a number at a keyboard may accidently type a space or two before the number so that, for example, we had space space 5638 instead of simply 5638. It would be nice to accept this as valid, because it would look numeric on the screen. Such leading spaces could be removed before the 'Check for numeric' procedure was entered. It would be necessary to count the spaces before the first non-blank character and then shift all the non-blanks along or down the array the appropriate number of positions. You might like to try your hand at doing the design for that, now.

A signed integer

If a sign is needed, then one way to allow for it would be to alter the initial inspection which is made to see if all the characters are numeric. Before inspecting the first character, set a flag, which could be called *Sign-flag*, to 'P' (for positive). If the first character is a digit, proceed as before. If it is a '+' sign, replace it by a zero. If it is a '–' sign, replace it by zero, but also set *Sign-flag* to 'N'. If the first character is anything else, reject it as before.

When the algorithm in Fig. 8.7 has been completed, inspect *Sign-flag*. If it is 'N', multiply *O-number* by –1.

A number with a decimal point (unsigned)

This is more complicated. One way of proceeding is as follows. During the initial inspection, allow a point '.', as well as digits, as a valid character. Then, if the input string is valid (that is, consists only of digits and points), count the points. If there is more than one, fail the input; otherwise continue as follows.

1. Find the length of the string (i.e. the position of the right-most digit, before the spaces start). Store this in *In-top*.
2. Find the position of the point. Store this in *In-pos*.
3. Transfer digits before the point into corresponding positions in an array of integers as was done with action 5 above.
4. Don't transfer the point.
5. Transfer the digits after the point into the array of integers, but one place to the left.
6. Multiply and add, as with actions 8, 6, 7 and 9 above.
7. Multiply the sum by 10 raised to the power of –1(in-top – in-pos)

An example will make clear the way this works.

A number, say 5.638, is keyed in to *In-arr*, and the more language-specific part of the program determines that, in *In-arr*, there are only digits and a single point before the spaces start. So the arrays are now as shown in Fig. 8.8. The point is searched for and found to be in element 2. The value 2 is assigned to *In-pos*. A space is searched for in *In-arr*, and it is discovered that the last digit is in position 5. So

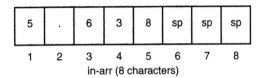
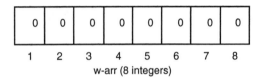

Figure 8.8

Top is assigned the value 5. Assignment of the first 5 characters is done, under the following conditions.
If sub < in-pos, then let w-arr[sub] = in-arr[sub]
If sub = in-pos, then do nothing
If sub > in-pos, then let w-arr[sub-1] = in-arr[sub]

The arrays appear as shown in Fig. 8.9.

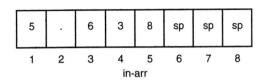
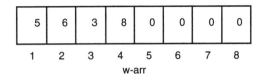

Figure 8.9

As before, each digit needs multiplying by a power of 10 depending on its position.
w-arr[1] multiplied by 10^3,
w-arr[2] multiplied by 10^2,
w-arr[3] multiplied by 10^1, and
w-arr[4] multiplied by 10^0 (as 10^0 is 1, that will not change it).

To control the repetition that does this, a new *Top* will be needed, calculated by

let top = top – 1

The arrangement in Fig. 8.10 is obtained.

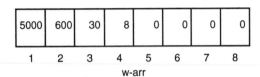

Figure 8.10

Summing these gives 5630, of course.
In-top = 5. In-pos = 2. Therefore (in-top – in-pos) = 3.
Multiplying 5630 by 10 raised to the power –3 gives 5.630, which is the number that was keyed in.
A modification of the design for the unsigned integer, above, will do all this, as follows.

Action list

1. let in-arr[sub] = space
2. let w-arr [sub] = 0
3. let top = 8
10. let in-pos = sub
4. let top = sub – 1
5. let w-arr[sub] = in-arr[sub]

Note that there is a change of type here, and in Pascal and Basic, a function will have to be used in place of a simple assignment.

11. let w-arr[sub] = in-arr[sub – 1]
6. let power = top – sub
12. let top = top – 1
7. let w-arr[sub] = w-arr[sub] $* 10^{power}$
8. let o-number = 0
9. add w-arr[sub] to o-number
13. compute power = –1$*$(top – in-pos).
14. compute o-number = o-number $* 10^{power}$

Condition list

C1 (until) sub > top
   F1 sub from 1 by 1
C2 (until) sub > top OR in-arr[sub] = space
   F2 sub from 1 by 1
C3 (until) sub > top
   F3 sub from 1 by 1
C4 in-arr[sub] = '.'
C5 sub < in-pos
C6 sub > in-pos

See Fig. 8.11.

You should now attempt Exercise 8.1 at the end of the chapter.

Further checks

Besides checking that an input is numeric, programs can **vet** input in other ways: to see if an input is too large or too small, or whether it is one of list of valid possibilities. As an example, consider a high-class shoe shop, where sales are not high volume. To activate the till, which is a Point Of Sale computer terminal, the assistant must key in

His/her number   in the **range** 20 to 69 inclusive, but 69 is a 'rogue' and is just used to end the program.

Stock number of shoe 5 digits. The last is a check digit.
Method of payment   one letter, C, Q, D or R.

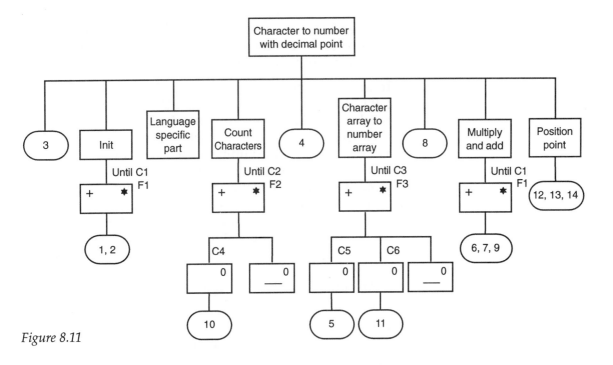

Figure 8.11

Amount tendered	Whole pence, maximum 19999.
'Z', or just Enter	'Z' cancels the whole set of inputs.
	Enter alone accepts them.

If the set of inputs is accepted, the computer prints an entry on the tillroll, otherwise it does nothing. (Note: In reality the stock file would be accessed and updated, but that is not relevant to a validation exercise.)

If any input is not acceptable, a short message appears on the display panel, and the assistant has to re-key. With stock number, it may be impossible to key the number correctly, if it is misprinted. In that case, 0000 is keyed and after all the inputs have been accepted, the 'Z' is keyed to cancel. 'Z' can also be used if, for example, it is realized that method of payment was wrong (e.g. 'D' instead of 'C') while amount is being keyed. If the assistant number 69 is keyed, a prompt 'Are you sure? (Y/N) ' appears. 'Y' then ends the program. Anything else causes a reprompt for assistant number.

In creating a design for the validation, it will be assumed that two subroutines are available. The first, Get-int, gets a valid number from the keyboard. To it are passed

(a) the first prompt to be used,
(b) the **error message**/subsequent prompt,
(c) the lowest number acceptable
(d) the largest number acceptable.

Get-int re-prompts until a valid integer, in the range

specified, is received. The second subroutine, Get-check, is passed a four digit number and returns the check digit that ought to be in the fifth position.

To obtain the assistant's number all that is necessary is to call Get-int with the limits 20 and 69. To obtain the stock-number, it will be necessary to call Get-int and Get-check as a pair, repeatedly, until the check digit returned is the same as the fifth digit of the number keyed in. Get-check will have to be given the first four digits of what was keyed in, so some means will be required to split the number input into two parts. Amount tendered is simple: Get-int is used. Method of payment will not be helped by a subroutine. At the end of a set of inputs, if neither Q nor Z is keyed, it will be assumed that that all is well, so no validation will be necessary there.

An outline high level design for one set of inputs can now be drawn.

Variable list

ass-no	N	assistant number
confirm	X	Q, Z or just Enter
i-method	X	method of payment, C, Q, D or R

Action list

1. write prompt 'are you sure '
2. read confirm from keyboard
3. let ass-no = 00
4. let confirm = ' '
10. open output disk file
11. close disk file

Condition list

C1   ass-no = 69
C2   confirm = 'Y'
C4   check-character returned = fifth digit of stock number

For the diagram, see Fig. 8.12.

Provided that you have done Exercise 8.1, everything in the diagram has been explained except Separate, which will be language specific, Get-method, which needs refining and Z-or-enter, which also needs refining.

Get-method is straightforward and can be a simple adaptation of the outline design given for a numeric, at the beginning of this chapter.

Action list

5. write 'Key in method of payment (C, Q, D or R) '
6. read i-method

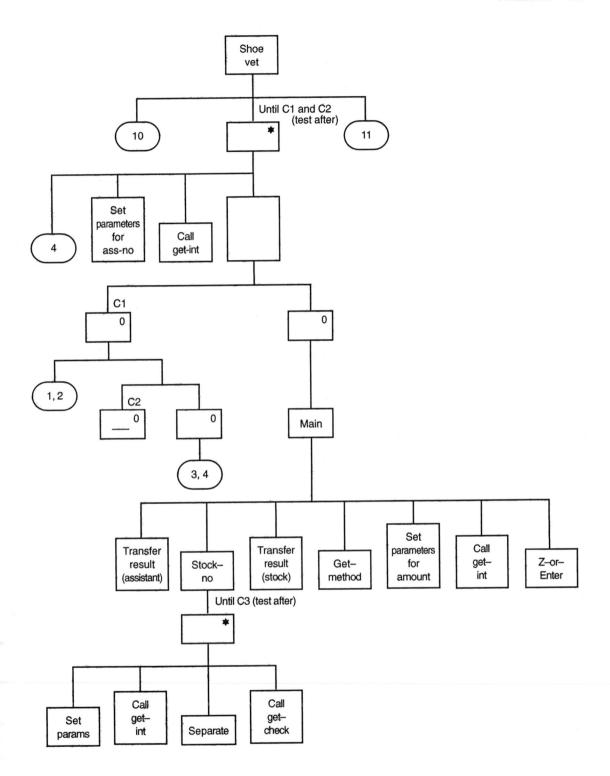

Figure 8.12

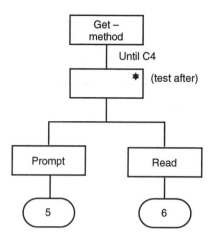

Figure 8.13

Condition list

C4 i-method = 'C' OR 'Q' OR 'D' OR 'R'

Z-or-enter determines whether the anything is to be written to the till roll or not. Suppose 'Z', if keyed, goes into the field called *Confirm*, used previously, and set to a space.

Action list

7. write 'Enter to confirm, Z to abandon'
8. read confirm
9. write four input fields to till roll

Condition list

C5 confirm = 'Z'
See Fig. 8.14.

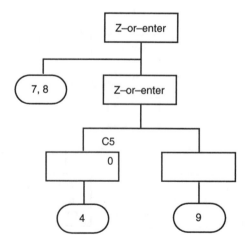

Figure 8.14

Exercises 8

8.1 Design a sub-program that incorporates the design in the chapter, called Character-to-integer-conversion, but which in addition accepts a prompt and a range, and then repeats until an integer in the given range is obtained. For example, if the sub-program is given the prompt 'Key Staff Number' and the values 20 and 69, it repeats and reprompts until a number in the range 20 to 69 is keyed.

8.2 Explain in detail the alterations that would need to be made to the design of 'Character to number with decimal point' in the chapter, to enable it to deal with a sign. The sign, if present should be the first character. Valid inputs would be 45, –3.67, +678, 3.142, 100, 100.01, –1.

8.3 Design a program that will deal with input and validation for the following situation.

A clerk at a meteorological office must key in observations obtained by phone from a number of weather stations. The fields to be keyed are:

Station name	Up to 15 characters; minimum of 4 non-blanks.
Min temperature	integer in range –20 to +35
Max temperature	integer in range –20 to +45, and greater than or equal to Min temperature.
Wind speed	integer in range 0 to 130
Wind direction	integer in range 0 to 359
Visibility	one of: B, P, F or G
Hours sunshine	two places of decimals, in range 0.00 to 22.00

If the operative realizes that an error has been made when it is too late to use the backspace key, she/he must be able to abandon the whole record and start again.

Valid sets of data should be written to disk. A station name of XXXX should end the program. As much use as possible should be made of the routines developed in the chapter.

8.4* An agricultural researcher gathers data about sugar beet growing in the fields of certain farmers. She visits the farms in late summer. Some of the data she gets from the farmer and some from measurements taken in a sample area in the field. The data is keyed directly into a portable computer she carries with her. The program validates the data as she inputs it. The fields and the validation criteria are:

Farm name	Non-blank
Field size in hectares	Range 5.0 to 99.9
Sowing date	Format: day and month, both as figures. Ignore leap years. Month must be in range 3 to 6.

Today's date	Format as for sowing date. Month must be at least 2 more than month in sowing date.
Fertiliser applied (kg)	Numeric integer less than 500.
Pesticide applied (litres)	Numeric integer less than 75.
Number of beets pulled	Numeric in range 1 to 10.
Total weight of pulled beets (kg)	Numeric and less than 50 with one place of decimals.

Design a program that will accept this input, validating it field by field as it is input and writing complete records to a file. A farm name of XXXX should terminate the program.

If the operative realizes that an error has been made when it is too late to use the backspace key, she/he must be able to abandon the whole record and start again.

As much use as possible should be made of the routines developed in the chapter.

9

Program design language (PDL)

The structure diagram, with its attendant variable and condition lists, is not the only way of getting a program algorithm down on paper. An alternative is to write the solution in program design language, often known as PDL, and sometimes as **pseudocode**. Some programmers prefer this to structure diagrams. It is not anything like so graphic or visual, and does not have the advantages that many of us gain from pictures, diagrams and graphs. One danger for the student is that it can look very like Pascal, and give him or her the feeling that in using it one is just coding the program twice. This can lead to the feeling that it is more or less a waste of time, and one might as well just get on and write the program.

When a program has been coded in a language such as Pascal, C, Cobol or Basic, it has to be translated into machine code. Machine code is all in binary, that is, all zeros and ones, but it is all that any computer can actually follow, in the the last analysis. This translation is done by a program, usually a **compiler**. The compiler, being only a progam, has no common sense and little flexibility. As a result the code has to be written to a very tight set of rules and go into a lot of fiddly detail. PLD avoids the tight rules and the distracting details and allows the designer to concentrate on the logic and the problem to be solved.

Machine code is bound up with the hardware and is called a **low level** language. Assembler is also a low level language. When a programming language gets further from the machine and nearer to the user's wants and needs, it is called a **high level** language. C is a medium level language. Cobol is a high level language. Fourth generation languages (4GLs) are even higher and so is PDL.

The level of PDL is too high for any compiler. The idea is to leave out the details, such as those necessary to deal with the format of the output, but to the retain what is fundamental: that is, the logic. There is some visual element: **indentation** is used to emphasise the selections and repetitions. Indentation means starting lines of writing a certain distance from the left margin, in a measured, systematic way. You will see examples of it later in this chapter.

Keywords and rules

We shall first write in, PDL, a design from an earlier chapter, and then point out the features. This will be followed by a list of keywords and rules. Keywords are mainly verbs you have already met, such as let, read, write, if, else and repeat. The design chosen is the one from Exercises 3.3 and 4.2: Design a program that will read two numbers from the keyboard and subtract the smaller from the larger, and keep on doing that until the user enters 'N' to the question 'Another pair (Y/N)'.

The solution given was:

Variable list

first_no
second_no
answer
again

Action list

1. write 'Key in a number'
2. read first_no
3. read second_no
4. let answer = first_no - second_no
5. let answer = second_no - first_no
6. write answer
7. write 'Another pair (Y/N)? '
8. read again

Condition list

C1 first_no > second_no
C2 again <> 'Y'

For the diagram, see Fig. 9.1.

This could be written in PDL as:

Variable list

first_no
second_no
answer
again

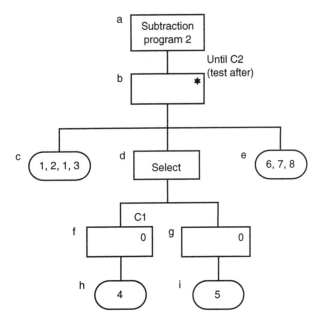

Figure 9.1

```
PROGRAM subtraction_program_2
 REPEAT
     WRITE 'Key in a number'
     READ first_no
     WRITE 'Key in a number'
     READ second_no
     IF first_no > second_no THEN
         LET answer = first_no - second_no
     ELSE
         LET answer = second_no - first_no
     ENDIF
     WRITE answer
     WRITE 'Another (Y/N)'
     READ again
 UNTIL again <> 'Y'
ENDPROGRAM
```

Observations

The words in capitals are **keywords**. The variables are in lower case. The repeated code comes in between the words REPEAT and UNTIL, and, because the test is made *after* each repetition, it is written at the end, after the word UNTIL. This repeated code is **indented**, four places to the right. This is an important visual clue to the reader (and one important reader is the writer). The selection is achieved by an IF...THEN...ELSE, as in most programming languages. The condition follows the word IF, and is followed by the word THEN. The word ELSE is on a line of its own. The selection is ended with the word ENDIF. Actions to be done when the condition is true are on the line or lines below the IF, and indented four places to the right. They are terminated by the word ELSE or the word ENDIF. Actions to be done when the condition is false are on the line or lines below the ELSE, and indented four places to the right. If there are several they are terminated by the word ENDIF. The word ELSE may be absent, if nothing is to be done in the event of the condition being false. Again, the layout and the indentation are essential visual clues to the reader, and must follow the rules.

These rules are only typical ones. There are no standards for PDL, and each book or programming department sets down its own rules. The variations are not very great, though, and if you follow the rules given in this chapter you will be in good company. For any one design, it is essential to follow one set of rules *consistently*, otherwise vagueness and doubt will creep in, and there must be no vagueness or doubt in a program design.

To recap on keywords, those used were, in alphabetical order,

ELSE	ENDIF	ENDPROGRAM	ELSE	IF
LET	PROGRAM	READ	REPEAT	
THEN	UNTIL	WRITE		

Some rules not covered in the very simple example above are:

- Subroutines begin with the word SUBPROGRAM, instead of the word PROGRAM.
- They end with the word ENDSUBPROGRAM.
- A subroutine is started, or skipped to, by the word CALL, followed by the name of the subprogram.
- Control is assumed to return to the instruction after the CALL as soon as the end of the subprogram is reached.
- A repetition that ends when a condition becomes true, and is tested before each repeat (Until with Before) is started by DO UNTIL condition, and ended by ENDDO.
- A repetition that continues while a condition remains true, and is tested before each repeat (While with Before) is started by DO WHILE condition, and ended by ENDDO.

Example

To illustrate some of these points, the problem in Chapter 7 about the traffic census (Fig. 7.3) will be shown using PDL.

As a result of a traffic census, a file called census_file was created, with one record for each vehicle. Among the fields in each record were vehicle_type and number of passengers carried. The vehicle_types were '1' for a car, '2' for a bus or coach and '3' for any other vehicle. The end of the file was marked by a record with '9' in vehicle_type. The output required was: the percentage of passengers that travelled by car, and the percentage of passenger_carrying vehicles that were cars. (All the occupants of cars were assumed to be passengers. Vehicle_type '3' vehicles were assumed to be carrying no passengers.)

Variable lists

Input

All input fields are part of a record called in_rec

i_type

i_no_pass

Output

Record name out_rec

o_pc_pass_car

o_pc_car

Calculations

o_pc_pass_car will be (total number of passengers in type 1 vehicles) / (total number of passengers) * 100.

o_pc_car will be (total number of type 1 vehicles) / (total number of type 1 vehicles + total number of type 2 vehicles) * 100.

As a result, the work variables will be as follows:

Work variables

w_1_count	counts type '1' vehicles
w_2_count	counts type '2' vehicles
w_car_pass	counts passengers in type '1' vehicles
w_total_pass	counts passengers in any type of vehicle

Each of the work variables will need to be initialized to zero.

```
PROGRAM  traffic_census
  OPEN files
  LET w_1_count, w_2_count, w_car_pass,
      w_total_pass = 0
  READ record from census file
  CALL body
  CALL foot
ENDPROGRAM

SUBPROGRAM body
  DO UNTIL i_type = 9
      ADD i_no_pass TO w_car_pass
```

```
            IF i_type = '1' THEN
                ADD 1 to w_1_count
                ADD i_no_pass to w_car_pass
            ELSE
                IF i_type = '2' THEN
                    ADD 1 TO w_2_count
                ENDIF
            ENDIF
            READ record from census_file
    ENDDO
ENDSUBPROGRAM
SUBPROGRAM foot
  LET o_pc_pass_car
        = w_car_pass / w_total_pass * 100
  LET o_pc_car
        = w_1_count / (w_1_count + w_2_count) * 100
  WRITE o_pc_pass_car
  WRITE o_pc_car
  CLOSE files
ENDSUBPROGRAM
```

The list of keywords has now become:

ADD   CALL   CLOSE   DO   ELSE
ENDDO   ENDIF   ENDPROGRAM
ENDSUBPROGRAM ELSE   IF   LET
OPEN   PROGRAM   READ   REPEAT
SUBPROGRAM   THEN   UNTIL   WRITE

Others that may be necessary are FOR, FROM and BY.

Exercises 9

Questions without answers are marked with a *.

9.1   Rewrite, in PDL, the design of the subprogram called 'T', shown in chapter 5, by Fig. 5.5 and its associated lists.

9.2   Rewrite, in PDL, the design of the subprogram called Find-check-ch, shown in Chapter 6, by Fig. 6.10 and its associated lists.

9.3*   Rewrite, in PDL, the design of the subprogram called Shoe vet, shown in Chapter 8, by Fig. 8.12 and its associated lists.

9.4*   Design, using PDL, a program to display the cost of a telephone call as it proceeds. The program should accept from a keyboard a charge band: L, A, B1 or B, and a time band: P, S or C. It should then wait, so that when the called person answers, Enter can be pressed. Timing is to start as soon as Enter is pressed.

The output, shown on the screen, should be

The cost of the call so far;
The number of seconds remaining on the current unit;
The length of the call so far in minutes and seconds.

When the call ends, pressing Enter should cause the timing to stop and the figures on the screen to 'freeze'.
The rates are as follows:

One unit costs 5.06 pence inclusive of VAT.

Time purchased for one unit: (s = sec)

	C	S	P
L	8 min	2 min	1 min 30 s
A	2 min 24 s	45 s	30 s
B1	1 min	20 s	15 s
B	48 s	16 s	12 s

Make the following assumptions. A subprogram called SYSTIME is available. This, when called, places the time since the computer was switched on, in seconds, into a variable called *Timein*.

10

Starting at the top: Tackling a project sized program

At the beginning of the book, in Chapter 1, a problem was set out, and you were told that by the end of the book you would be able to draw up a design for that problem. It is given here, in this chapter, and is reinforced by another, similar example. The designs incorporate many of the techniques covered in earlier chapters, namely

- Nested repetitions
- The concept of head–body–foot
- Reading a file into an array
- Writing a file
- A repetition with test before
- A repetition with test after
- A FOR repetition
- Getting data with 'read ahead'
- Getting data without 'read ahead'
- Getting a response with confirmation ('are you sure?')
- Searching an array

On an office wall was a picture of a small furry animal scratching its head. Underneath, the caption said, 'When at last I'd got it all together, I forgot where I'd put it.' Poor little chap. We know exactly how he feels. With so many problems in real life, the difficulty lies in their sheer size, and in knowing where to begin. When a problem is small you can hold the whole thing in your head at once – the various factors, the outcome you want, the one you don't want, the risks, and a possible solution. When the problem is big, it is easy to let some of these slip and soon you are in a muddle. In this chapter you will be shown, by way of examples, how to begin and how to get everything down on paper in an orderly way, so that muddle is avoided.

As all programming problems are different, there is no single set of rules that can be followed mechanically. But there are definitely simple guides that can be learned and used to advantage. The use of them will be illustrated by the creation of a solution to the problem of the supermarket till, stated in Chapter 1, and re-stated, for convenience, here.

The supermarket checkout

The program simulates a supermarket checkout.

Inputs

1. At start of day, a stock-and-prices file is read into a table in main store. This file has, for each kind of good, many fields, but the only ones read into main store are:
   stock number (4 digits + check digit)
   description (15 characters)
   price (in pence, max 9999)
   quantity in stock (an integer, max 5000)
   Also obtained, via the operating system or the keyboard, is the date.
2. As each checkout clerk comes on duty, she keys in an identification number (an id). These are preceded by the letter I.
3. At end of day, the letter E is keyed. Confirmation is asked for, and given by the letter Y.
4. For each item purchased, a stock number. This actually comes from a bar-code scanner, but you can simulate it by keying in a 5 digit 'self-checking' number.
5. For each customer, a method of payment and an amount tendered, preceded by the number 2, keyed instead of a stock number. The date and the time will also be used. If possible, both should come from the operating system, but if your programming language does not have the facilities for accessing them, they may be simulated as follows: the date is keyed in at the beginning of the day, when the program is first loaded. Time is not used. Instead, each customer is given a serial number, starting from one when each clerk comes on duty.

The methods of payment will be C for cash, Q for cheque, R for credit card, or D for debit card. Amount tendered will be in pence.

Outputs

For each customer, printed on paper, a receipt showing

- the shop name, Freshfare
- the name and price of each item purchased
- a total amount due
- an item count
- the amount tendered
- the change due
- the date, the clerk's id, and either the time or a serial no.

On screen, the price, as each item is 'scanned'. As soon as a customer's bill is totalled, the amount due replaces this on the screen.

In main store (not a real output, but a simulated one), an update to the quantity in stock for each item from the stock file, in main store.

On disk

- A total of the value of sales, and number of items for each operative, for her stint or shift
- A total of the value of sales, and number of items for the day, before the program is terminated, on close of business.
- The prices file, written back at the end of the day, with the updated quantities on it.

Processing

Most of the processing needed is obvious from the descriptions of the input and output. The check digit on the stock number is calculated as follows. The digits are weighted, the check digit itself having a weight of one, and the leftmost digit a weight of 5. Each digit is multiplied by its weighting, and the resulting products are added. The resulting total is divided by 11. The remainder should be zero. If it is not, the number is invalid. The cashier can then try again. (Numbers that would require a check digit of 10 are not used.)

The specification

In commercial practice, where both systems analysts and programmers are employed, the analysts will usually have thrashed out every detail of what is wanted, with the users. The programmer should find that the specification is complete. The first job, surprisingly difficult sometimes, is to understand it, fully. With a project, the specification may be incomplete. It may have to be added to here and there, or even altered a little, as one goes along. So that this can be illustrated, the problem above has been made deliberately imprecise in places.

The best way to be sure you that you really do know what the program is supposed to do is to create a very small amount of test data, and write down the expected results.

For the shop till problem we need at least two operatives, and one of them needs at least two customers, and one of the customers needs to buy at least two items. The following prices file would be enough.

Reference	Description	Price	Quantity
12343	IBCOL	0073	0050
68217	SOYA MILK	0079	0222
12122	BRAN CEREAL	0122	1000
36633	HOUMOUS	0075	0002
77771	P/APPLE SLICES	0041	2222
28150	BAKED BEANS	0017	5000

- Program starts up. Date is 15/07/94
- Operative 28 comes on duty.
- Customer 1 buys baked beans, and tenders £1.00. Customer 2 buys Ibcol and houmous, and tenders £5.00
- Operative 09 takes over.
- Customer 3 buys pineapple slices and soya milk and tenders £1.20.
- Program closes down for the day.

The till roll should be as shown in Fig. 10.1.

The screen messages and prompts should also be written out, and so should the final appearance of the prices file.

The data: structure, names, data types

Every program is concerned with producing useful output from the available input. The first step, therefore, is to become familiar with the data, and its structure. Take three pieces of scrap paper, and head them INPUT, OUTPUT and WORK FIELDS (or WORKING VARIABLES). Using the programming language you have chosen, list every variable or data item you are going to need, together with its data type (in COBOL the PIC). Where records are needed, show this. Use names that are meaningful, but not so long as to be clumsy. Group together items that go together, under suitable headings, and use prefixes to show the group identity.

Recently, the author was called to help a student struggling with a validation program. Valid data was being deliberately assigned to fields prefixed 'bad-', and invalid data to fields prefixed 'good-'. No wonder he was struggling! He wasn't a fool. He had made a typing error at some point and then had to make corrections. The contradictory naming had just 'happened', and he thought it would be too much trouble to put it right. He was mistaken there – it would have been worth every minute. Meaningful data names (variables) are *essential*, because muddle is your biggest enemy.

A good way to get going on the data is to make lists of variables. They probably won't be complete at the first try, but never mind – it's the thought that counts. In what follows,

Line

```
        FRESHFARE              3
                               4
-------------------------      5
                      £        6
    BAKED BEANS     0.17       7
                               8
TOTAL             0.17         9
          1 ITEMS             10
CASH    1.00                  11
CHANGE DUE        0.83        12
-------------------------     13
THANK YOU FOR SHOPPING        14
       AT FRESHFARE           15
94/07/15 ID 28 SR NO 001      16
                              17
-------------------------      1
                               2
        FRESHFARE              3
                               4
-------------------------      5
                      £        6
    IBCOL         0.50
    HOUMOUS       0.75
TOTAL             1.25
          2 ITEMS
CASH    5.00
CHANGE DUE        3.75
-------------------------
THANK YOU FOR SHOPPING
       AT FRESHFARE
94/07/15 ID 28 SR NO002
-------------------------
        FRESHFARE
-------------------------
                      £
-------------------------     18
TOTAL FOR OPERATOR    28      19
TOTAL             1.59        20
          3 ITEMS             21
-------------------------
```

```
        FRESHFARE
-------------------------
                      £       .
    P/APPLE SLICES  0.41
    SOYA MILK       0.79
TOTAL             1.20
          2 ITEMS
CASH    1.20
CHANGE DUE        0.00
-------------------------
THANK YOU FOR SHOPPING
       AT FRESHFARE
94/07/15 ID 09 SR NO001
-------------------------
        FRESHFARE
-------------------------
                      £
-------------------------
TOTAL FOR OPERATOR    09
TOTAL             1.20
          2 ITEMS
-------------------------
        FRESHFARE
-------------------------
                      £
-------------------------
TOTAL FOR OPERATOR    00
TOTAL             2.79
          5 ITEMS
-------------------------
```

Figure 10.1 The till roll

explanations that would not normally be written down are in *italics*.

In the example, there is:

- the short name that will be used in the program
- the data type denoted as in earlier chapters
- an explanation, if the short name is not totally clear.

The explanations in italics are an indication of the thinking that would precede the writing of the entries.

The codes used for data types are: NI for numeric integer, ND for numeric-with-decimal, X for string, C for character and B for Boolean. These were introduced in Chapter 5.

Input from file

First, there is the data from the stock-and-prices file, which is in the form of records with the following structure:

stock-no	stock number, including check digit,	NI
desc	description	X
price	selling price per item, in pence	NI
quant	quantity in stock	NI

Note: these records will in practice contain many other fields such as On-order-flag and Supplier-reference, but these are being ignored because they will not affect the design.

Input from keyboard

There are items keyed by the operative at start of day and start or end of a work-session:

k-date	?	today's date. Format will depend on system used
k-operator-id	NI	till operative's identification nmbr
k-op-indic	C	E for end of day; I for change of operative; Enter key alone for continue
k-confirm	C	Y or N. Used to confirm entry of E, which ends operations for the day

There are items keyed by the operative during the course of serving a customer (including what would in reality come from a bar-code reader):

k-stock-no	NI	stock number from bar code reader (or keyboard in this simulation)
k-method	C	method of payment. A letter. Q for cheque, C for cash, D for debit card, R for credit card
k-amount	NI	amount tendered by customer, input as pence

The three integers from the keyboard, k-stock-no, k-amount and k-operator-id, will not actually be input as integers. They will all be obtained in the same way, via a call to the subroutine that gets and validates. It could be argued, therefore, that they are not truly input, but working variables. It is a matter of choice which list you put them in, or maybe a matter of when and how they occur to you. The input string used by them all will be:

k-string	X	the input string for an integer, before validation

Output to printer (till roll/receipt)

The items listed here could vary depending on the language to be used. With COBOL we would need a long list, as the editing is accomplished by means of moves to the items in the records that make up the print lines. In Pascal and C, few extra variables are necessary. Listed here, therefore, is the minimum that would be necessary when using Pascal, assuming that the texts of messages have been coded as constants. Variables such as price, which are in the array of prices, or the date, which is in the input, are not repeated. Total fields will be needed, for the customer totals that go on the receipts, and for the control totals on each operative's session and on the till for the day. Three fields are therefore needed to total the prices, and three more to count the items:

o-cust-total	NI	total of customer's bill, as pence
o-op-total	NI	total money taken by current operative so far
o-day-total	NI	total money taken at this till so far today
o-cust-items	NI	number of items bought by current customer
o-op-items	NI	number of items checked by current operative so far
o-day-items	NI	number of items checked through this till so far today

Other variables that will be needed are:

o-change	NI	change due to customer
o-ser-no	NI	serial number of customer for this operative. Starts from 1 when operative signs on

The change due will not of course have the appearance of an integer when it is actually printed, but its conversion to pounds is not a matter for program design.

The receipt heading, as lines 1–6 in Fig.10.1, will be needed for every customer, and for every set of control totals (in this latter case as a spacer, so that the piece of paper is big enough to tear off and put in the till).

Output to the screen

All items output to the little screen at the till are also printed, so no additional variables are needed.

Output to the disk

The same applies. The output to the disk is a copy of some of what goes onto the till roll. It goes to disk so that it can be processed by other programs which do accounting and analysis.

Working variables

prices-array		A record with the same structure as that on the input file. Occurs 100 times in this simulation.
stock-no		
desc		
price		
quant		
w-max	NI	The number of records on the file will not be the same each day, so the array will not be completely filled. The number read in can be stored, to limit searching.
sub		Subscript for handling the prices-array.
sub1		Subscripts for manipulating the input string when getting a valid integer from the keyboard.
sub2	}	
sub3		
w-string	X	string to which input string is moved, character by character, during validation.
w-integer		integer to which string above is converted.
w-upper	NI	the largest value the integer may have.
w-lower	NI	the smallest value the integer may have.
w-sum	NI	the sum of the products of the digits and their weightings, when checking a stock number
w-rem	NI	the remainder after division by 11
w-quotient	NI	the answer or quotient after integer division by 11.

Part 2 The main activities

Having made a start with the data, the next step is to try to write down what the main parts of the program will be. These may end up as procedures or groups of procedures (Pascal), or major functions (C), or paragraphs or groups of paragraphs (Cobol). No attempt will be made to arrange them or to go into detail. The style will be informal.

A. Reading the file into the array in main store. Storing the number of records read, in *W-max*. Getting the date. Zeroing all the totals.

B. Changing shifts at the till: printing and writing to file the totals for the operative leaving; on the till roll, printing the headings, getting the i.d. of the operative arriving; resetting the serial number to 0. Zeroing the operative totals. Clearing the indicators *K-op-indic* and *K-confirm* to spaces.

C. Passing items over the bar-code reader: i.e. attempting to get the stock-numbers and prices of one customer's goods. For each item, this will involve: doing the arithmetic for the self-checking of the stock number; re-prompting if the number is invalid; searching the array for a match; providing an error message if the item is not found.

D. 'Processing' an item once the price is found: subtracting one from quantity in stock and adding into all six total fields. Note that it will be necessary, if doing a project, to consider what is to be done if a customer presents an item which has a stock number that really is not on the prices file. In reality there would have to be some way of selling the item. For simplicity, it will be assumed, for now, that this complication does not arise.

E. Getting a payment method and payment from the customer, and providing change and a receipt. Zeroing customer totals.

F. End of day recording to paper and disk, of totals for the till (with headings on the till roll). Writing the file (with its updated stock figures) back onto the disk.

G. Subsidiary to the above: getting valid integers for operative i.d., stock number and amount tendered. When called, this routine will be given the minimum and maximum values that the integer may have, and will return a numeric integer in that range from the keyboard.

Part 3 The main repetitions

It is now time to identify the main repetitions. This is a short step, but absolutely vital. At the till, during the day, there is a succession of operatives: operative repeats. Each operative has many customers: customer after customer after customer: customer repeats. Each customer has a basket or trolley of items (goods), and item after item goes through: item repeats. We must also look at what stops these repetitions. For the operatives, it is keying E, followed by a confirming Y, at the end of the last shift ((k-op-indic = 'E') AND (k-confirm = 'Y')) i.e. C1 AND C2. As far as any one operative is concerned, the customers stop when the shift ends: on the keying of I or E when prompted for, just after a customer has been given a receipt: ((k-op-indic = 'I') OR (k-op-indic = 'E')) : C3 OR C1. The end of a customer is signalled by a stock-number of 2 or 00002: (k-stock-no = 2): C4.

Part 4 A first attempt at a high level diagram

Condition list

See the paragraph above. For the diagram, see Fig. 10.2.

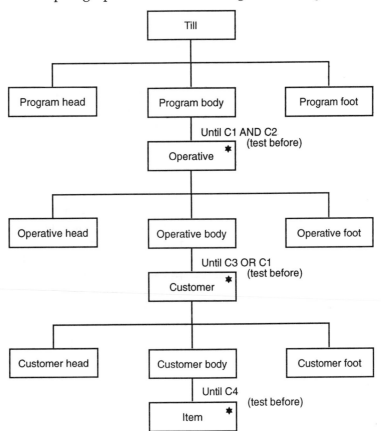

Figure 10.2

Part 5 Relating the main activities to the first-attempt diagram

Using the letters from Part 2 above, A clearly forms part if not all of Program_head. The first part of B goes into Operative_foot, but the second part of B goes into Operative_head. C and D form most of Item. E will be attached to Customer_foot. F will be in Program_foot.

As the logic is dependent on the value of *K-stock-no* and two indicators, *K-op-indic* and *k-confirm*, it is vital to decide where they are initialized to make the conditions true so that the repetitions can be entered, where they are altered so that the repetitions are terminated, and where they are reset so that the repetitions can be entered again.

Let us start at the bottom with Item. C4 depends on *K-stock-no*. This is obtained from the keyboard in Customer_head, so that Item can be entered, and obtained again in Item so that Item can be terminated.

Customer: C3 and C1 both refer to *K-op-indic*. This is obtained from the keyboard in Customer_foot. So that Customer can be entered or re-entered, it must be initialized/reset in Operative_head – to a space.

Operative: C1 refers to *K-op-indic* and C2 to *K-confirm*. *K-confirm* is obtained from the keyboard in Operative_Foot. To get into Operative, both must be initialized in Program_head: to spaces. Note that if *K-op-indic* is set to E but then *K-confirm* is set to anything other than Y, control goes to Operative_head, and should then go to Operative. *K-confirm* can be reset to spaces either in Operative_head, or just before it is obtained from the keyboard.

As has been shown in an earlier chapter, when getting data from a file or from a keyboard (or other input device) it is often necessary to 'read ahead', i.e. to attempt a read before entering the repetition where reads are mainly done. It is necessary here, and a 'get' of stock number must be done in Customer_head. The reason is that the entry of a stock number may not be successful. It may be printed wrongly on the packet or label, or be illegible, so that it will not pass the selfcheck. Or it may not be found in the array of prices and quantities. The operative must be able to abandon the attempt to input the number, and instead either start on the next one, or key 2.

A check through the above reveals that all the procedures on the 'first attempt' chart above are needed, and that there are no problems that will require its alteration.

Part 6 The refinements
Program_head_A

Action list

To read a record, the following will be needed:

1. read record from file into an element of prices-array
2. let sub = 1
3. add 1 to sub

Before the file can be read:

4. assign the input file
5. open the input file

When all the records have been read in:

6. close the input file.

This draws attention to the fact that the output files need assigning and opening, too:

7. assign the print file 'receipts'
8. open 'receipts'
9. assign the disk file 'totals'
10. open 'totals'
11. let w-max = sub – 1

For the date:

12. prompt for date if not obtainable from system
13. read k-date

Zeroing totals:

14. let o-cust-tot-total, o-op-tot-total, o-day-tot-total, o-cust-items, o-op-items, o-day-items
15. let k-op-indic, k-confirm = ' '

Condition list

C5 eof(input file)

See Fig. 10.3 for the diagram

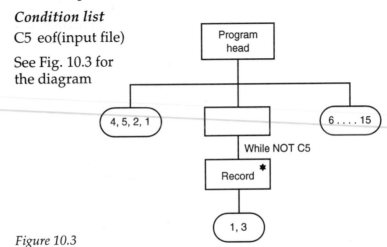

Figure 10.3

Operative_head

Action list

16. let k-op-indic, k-confirm = 0
17. let w-lower = 1
18. let w-upper = 98
19. let prompt = 'key in your operator i.d. '
20. let o-ser-no = 0
21. let o-op-total, o-op-items = 0

See Fig. 10.4 for
the diagram.

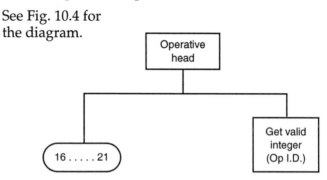

Figure 10.4

Operative
head

16 21

Get valid
integer
(Op I.D.)

Customer_head_B

The activities here are:
- getting a stock number. This is a two stage process. First a valid integer in range is obtained by setting up parameters and calling the subroutine Read_int. Second, a procedure to find whether it self-checks, called Digit_check, is called. These two need repeating until a valid stock number is obtained. So that the prompt can be changed after the first try, a read ahead is used. Both subroutines here are as developed in previous chapters: Read-int in Chapter 8 and Digit_check in Chapter 6.
- Adding one to the customer serial number;
- Starting off a receipt; a subroutine called Receipt_heading will be called to do this is. It is the printing of lines 1 to 6 of the receipt (see Fig.10.1). All the lines are literals.

Action list

22. let w-lower = 1
23. let w-upper = 99998
24. add 1 to o-ser-no

There is a repetition within Read int which ensures that a valid positive integer will emerge. Digit check has no safeguard. Therefore the condition will test the remainder from the division by 11 to see if it is zero.

Condition list

C6   w-rem <> 0

For the diagram, see Figs. 10.5 and 10.6.

Input stock no is drawn separately in Fig. 10.6 because it will be needed in Item as well as here.

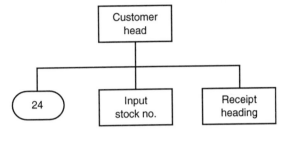

Figure 10.5

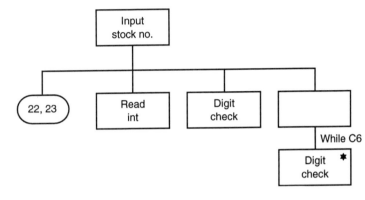

Figure 10.6

Receipt_heading

This is the printing of lines 1 to 6 of the receipt (see Fig.10.1). All the lines are literals.

Item C

This consists of:

- searching the array for the price etc
- if found, then adding to the total fields, subtracting one from quantity, displaying and printing the price; else displaying an error message.
- getting the stock-number from the next item.

Action list

For the 'if found':

25. add 1 to each of o-cust-items, o-op-items, o-day-items
26. add price[sub] to each of o-cust-total, o-op-total, o-day-total
27. subtract 1 from quant[sub]
28. write desc[sub] and price[sub] to printer
29. write desc[sub] and price[sub] to screen

For the 'else':

30. write 'item not on file'

Condition list

C7 If stock-no[sub] = k-stock-no

The refinement of Search_array will be exactly as in Chapter 5. A refined diagram is shown in Fig. 10.7.

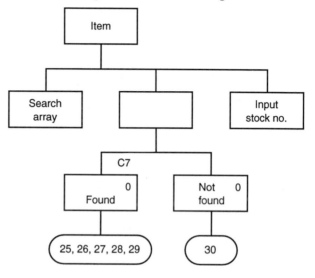

Figure 10.7

Customer_foot_E

Getting a payment method and a payment amount can usefully be put in a separate procedure from the printing of the end of the receipt. The end of the receipt will be lines 13–17 of Fig.10.1. Prompting for the indicator (and giving the option of just pressing enter), together with zeroing *O-cust-items* and *O-cust-total*, form the rest of this procedure.

Action list

31. let o-cust-items, o-cust-total = 0
32. write prompt 'if new op, key I, else enter'
33. read k-op-indic

An intermediate diagram for Customer_foot can now be drawn (Fig. 10.8).

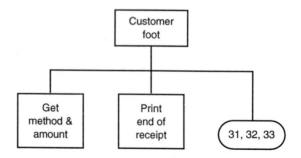

Figure 10.8

Get_method_and_amount

Getting the method can be a simple repetition with only one prompt and with the repetition test after. Getting the amount means setting up the prompt and the upper and lower limits, and calling Read_int. The lower limit should be total due. It is not mentioned in the specification, but highly unlikely that a customer will ever pay more than £600, so this gives an upper limit.

Action list

34. write prompt 'give method of payment (c, q, r or d) '
35. read k-method
36. let k-prompt = 'amount tendered? '
37. let lower = o-cust-total
38. let upper = 60000

Condition list

C8 k-method = 'c' OR 'q' OR 'r' OR 'd'

For the diagram, see Fig. 10.9.

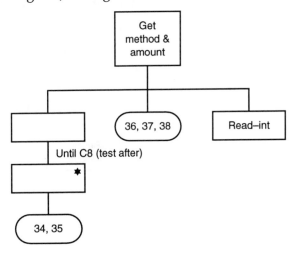

Figure 10.9

Print_end_of_receipt

This is a straightforward series of writes.

Action list

39. write o-cust-total to both screen and receipt
40. write o-cust-items
41. write k-amount
42. write (k-amount - o-cust-total)
43. write literals for lines 15, 16 and 17
44. write k-date, k-operator-id, o-ser-no

There are no conditions. A diagram would be a simple sequence of the above and is not worth drawing.

Operative_foot.B

The printing, writing to disk and zeroing are straightforward. The form of the printing will be as in Fig.10.1, lines 18–21. If the end of the shift was indicated with an E not an I, confirmation needs seeking. The prompt will be for Y or N but anything other than Y will be taken as meaning that the shift is not over, so reprompting will not be necessary.

Action list

45. write literal for line 19
46. write o-operator-id to receipt file
47. write o-op-total to receipt file
48. write o-op-items to receipt file
49. write o-operator-id, o-op-total, o-op-items to disk file
50. write prompt 'confirm end of day, Y/N '
51. read k-confirm
52. let o-op-total, o-op-items = 0

Condition list

C1 (again) k-op-indic = 'E'

For the diagram, see Fig. 10.10.

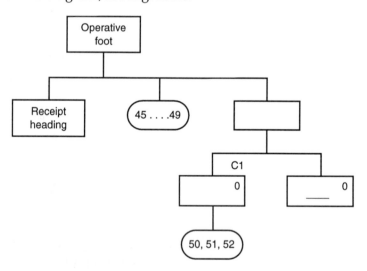

Figure 10.10

Program_foot.F

This is similar to Operative_foot, above, but simpler. The printing of the day totals is exactly the same as the printing of the operative totals except that the operative id is shown as 00.

Action list

53. write literal for line 19
54. let k-operator-id = 00

55. write o-operator-id
56. write o-day-total
57. write o-day-items
58. write o-operator-id, o-day-total, o-day-items to disk file 59. open prices file for writing
60. let sub = 1
61. add 1 to sub
62. write record prices-array[sub] to prices file
63. close all files

Condition list

C9 sub <= w-max

For the diagram, see Fig. 10.11.

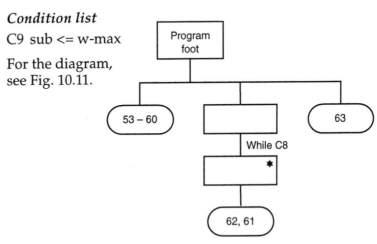

Figure 10.11

All that remains is the procedure to get a positive integer, Read_int. This was developed and discussed in Chapter 7. The design can now be dry run, and coded.

The Till example design was a little easier than normal, because parts had already been encountered before in earlier chapters. A second example will now be given, starting from scratch. It concerns multiple-choice testing.

A second example
Multiple choice testing

The problem is to design a program to present and mark multiple choice tests. The questions, together with the responses from which the candidate can choose, are to be kept on files on disk, one file for each test. Also on the file are the answers, the number of questions in the test, the pass mark and the time allowed.

Requirements

A test may have between seven and 40 questions. Each will give a choice of four answers, lettered a, b, c, d.

The candidate must start by entering his/her name and the reference code of the course. Candidates are then told how many questions there are, the pass mark and the time

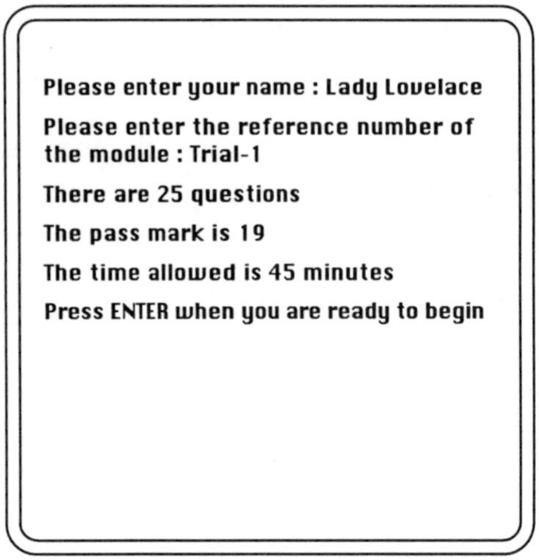

Please enter your name : Lady Lovelace

Please enter the reference number of the module : Trial-1

There are 25 questions

The pass mark is 19

The time allowed is 45 minutes

Press ENTER when you are ready to begin

Fig.10.12

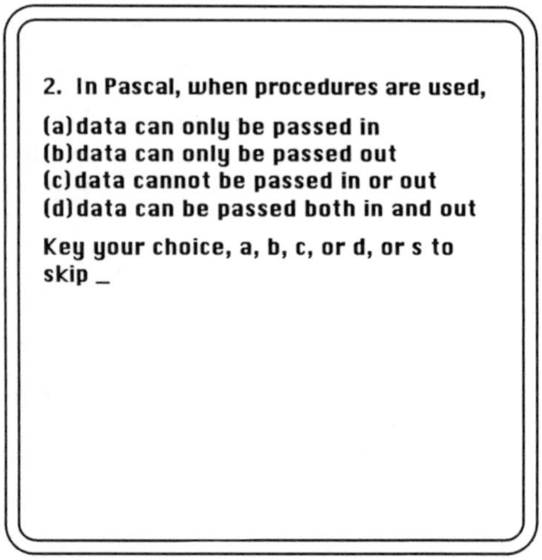

2. In Pascal, when procedures are used,

(a) data can only be passed in
(b) data can only be passed out
(c) data cannot be passed in or out
(d) data can be passed both in and out

Key your choice, a, b, c, or d, or s to skip _

Fig.10.13

allowed, and asked to press Enter when they want to begin. An example of how the screen would look at this point is shown in Fig.10.12

As soon as the candidate presses Enter, the program gets the time from the computer's clock. The program terminates the test when the time is up. The questions and possible answers are presented one at a time in sequence. The candidate may choose a, b, c, d or 'skip'. A typical screen is shown in Fig.10.13.

If the end of the test is reached before time is up, the candidate is given a choice: Stop, Review All, or Review Skips.

Choosing 'Review All' causes a return to question 1. The only difference being that the previous answer chosen is shown, and if 'skip' is then selected, this answer remains unchanged. Choosing 'Review Skips' causes just the skipped questions to be presented again.

When time runs out or Stop is selected, the program prints out the test name/code (from the file), the date (from the system), the candidate's name, the score, the pass mark, the verdict - pass or fail - the numbers of the questions that the candidate got wrong, and a complete list of the candidate's answers. Fig 10.14 illustrates this, but to save space it refers to a test with only three questions.

Understanding the problem

The specification has usefully shown both some inputs and some outputs. All that is really needed in addition is a picture of the beginning of the file. This is shown schematically below in Fig. 10.15. Its actual form will depend on the language used and the system:

```
Test: Trial-1
Date: 22.05.94
Candidate:   Lady Lovelace
Score:        2
Pass mark:   2
Verdict:      Pass


The numbers of the questions you got
wrong were: 3
end of list
List of your responses:
1 a
2 c
3 b
end of printout for this test
```

```
In Pascal, a compound statement is
usually delimited by

(a)  round brackets
(b)  curly brackets
(c)  begin and end
(d)  do and end
c      PAS-01   25   19   45

In Pascal, when procedures are used,

(a)  data can only be passed in
(b)  data can only be passed out
(c)  data cannot be passed in or out
(d)  data can be passed both in and out
d               00   00   00
```

Fig.10.14

Fig.10.15 The beginning of the multiple choice data file.

The solution

Part 1: the data

As always, it is best to start by thinking about the data, and this is done by making lists of variables. They probably won't be complete at the first try, but never mind – it's the thought that counts. In what follows, explanations that would not normally be written down are in *italics*.

Input from file

The main data will need to be in the form of records with the structure:

question	X	the question or lead-in to it
choice_a	X	the letter (a) and all the text that follows it
choice_b	X	
choice_c	X	
choice_d	X	
ans	C	just one letter - the right answer.

However, other data is needed too:

ref_code	X	Reference code identifying test
no_qs	NI	The number of questions in the test
pass_mark	NI	The pass mark
mins_allowed	NI	The time allowed, in minutes.

Ideally, (and easily if COBOL is being used), there should be be two record types. However it will be simpler to have these four 'other' fields in every record, and the space wasted will probably not matter. These fields need contain data in only the first record - in the others they can be empty (spaces and zeros).

Input from keyboard

i_name	X	The candidate's name
i_ref_code	X	The name of the module or test, as the candidate sees it (for checking)
i_resp	C	The candidate's answer or response to a question.
i_end_choice	C	The candidate's choice as to whether to review, try the skipped ones, or finish.

Input from operating system

It is assumed that the implementation of the language you intend to use has facilities for getting date and time from the operating system. Most do.

From calling the date:

i_yy	NI	The year
i_mm	NI	The month
i_dd	NI	The day

From calling the time:

i_hr	NI	The hour on 24 hour clock
i_min	NI	The minutes
i_sec	NI	The seconds

Output to screen

(Prompts and messages. These will be literals or constants.)
(The test questions and answers, but these will be as input, and so do not need renaming.)

o_resp	C	When reviewing, the response given previously

This gives rise to an important thought. Because the candidate must be able to go back to earlier questions and look at them again (review), most of the data from the file will be needed more than once. It will therefore be necessary to keep rereading the file from the disk, or to have the whole file in main store. Since the file will be small – not more than 20 k bytes – the second of these would be the easier option. We shall therefore need an array of records in main store, into which we can read the file. The record structure can be identical to that used in making the file. However, we also need to store all the responses, against the questions, as the user makes them. So we need:

o_resp   *array of C, occurring 40 times.*

Output to printer

Much of this will come from the inputs and the arrays of questions and answers already mentioned. In addition there will be:

w_score	NI	The number correct
w_verdict	X	The word Pass or the word Fail

Working variables

w_counter	NI	The number of the current question
w_end_secs	NI	The time the test will finish, as seconds from midnight
w_time_secs_now	NI	The time now, as seconds from midnight
w_secs_left	NI	The number of seconds remaining, before the test must stop
w_array		Array of Records, occurring 40 times. The array into which the whole test and its control information is to be read
subr	NI	Subscript used when filling the array from the file
subf	NI	Subscript used during final printing.

w_counter is also a subscript. It would probably be possible to manage with that one alone. It may make the design easier to follow if more than one is used.

Part 2 The main activities

A. Reading the file into the array in main store.
B. Getting the candidate's name etc at the start, and giving initial information on screen.
C. Getting the time when the user signals start, and working out the finishing time, in seconds from midnight.
D. Getting the time frequently, and working out how many seconds are left.

Making sure that the program stops letting the candidate give answers, after time is up, is going to be an important part of the program. A number of repetitions are going to be controlled by 'while time remains' or 'until time is up'. Once an instruction to get data from the keyboard has been reached (e.g. READ in Pascal, getch in C or ACCEPT in Cobol), the program waits for a response, and to override this when time was up would be difficult. We shall therefore adopt the principle used in 'Mastermind' 'I've started so I'll finish' – and allow the candidate to give a response if the prompt was given within the time allowed.

E. Displaying the questions one at a time and inviting a response – either an initial attempt at an answer, or an altered answer.
F. Displaying just the questions that were skipped previously.
G. Totting up the score, and comparing it with the pass mark.
H. Doing the final printing.
I. When a response has been obtained for the last question, giving the candidate a choice on what to do next.

Part 3 The main repetitions

It is now time to identify the main repetitions. This is a short step but absolutely vital. The obvious things that repeat are questions. The candidate attempts question after question after question. Therefore what repeats is: question. What stops this repetition? Answer: the candidate coming to the end of the questions, or running out of time. In other words, he or she continues while ((w_counter <= no_qs) and (w_secs_left > 0)). This will be (C1 AND C2).

When the candidate comes to the end of the questions and there is time left, he/she can go through the questions again, either to try the skipped ones or to check the answers chosen. So, provided the candidate is quick, he/she can go through the test again and again and again. This repetition, is at a higher level than the other. It comes to an end when the candidate chooses to end it by keying x, or time runs out. In other words, it continues while ((w_end_choice <> 'x') and (w_secs_left > 0)). This will be (C3 AND C2).

Part 4 A first attempt at a high-level diagram

See Fig. 10.16.

Part 5 Relating the main activities to the first-attempt diagram.

Using the letters from part 2 above, A, B and C clearly form part of Program_head, Program_foot will be mainly G and H. Test_foot will be mainly I, but D will probably be needed here too. It is clear that E and F are attached to Question in some way, but the allocation is not simple like the others. This is because Question works in two different ways. If the candidate is going through the test for the first time, or is reviewing all questions, *W_counter* will be incremented by one each time. But if he/she is going through only the questions that had been skipped, *W_counter* will have to be increased by whatever is necessary to reach the next skipped question. Question ought therefore to be two alternative

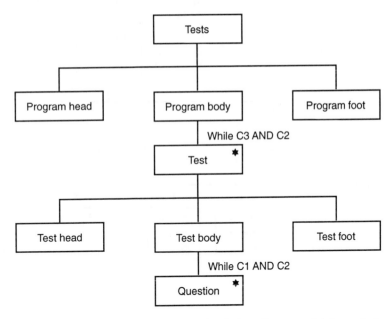

Figure 10.16

'Questions' which could be called Q-All – to which activities E and D would be attached – and Q-Skipped – to which activities F and D would be attached.

The condition for one will be (w_end_choice = 'r') - C4 - and for the other (w_end_choice = 's') - C5.

All the main activities have now been assigned to the chart, leaving Test_head with nothing. It looks as if Test_head can be dropped from the diagram.

Part 6 A second attempt at a diagram

See Fig. 10.17.

Assuming this diagram to be more or less correct, the main framework of the design is in place, and all that is needed now is refinement of the all the terminal boxes.

Part 7 The refinements

Read array (A).

Action list

1. read record from file into an element of w_array
2. let w_counter = 1
3. add 1 to w_counter
4. assign the input file
5. open the input file
6. close the input file

Condition list

C4 eof(input file)

See Fig. 10.18

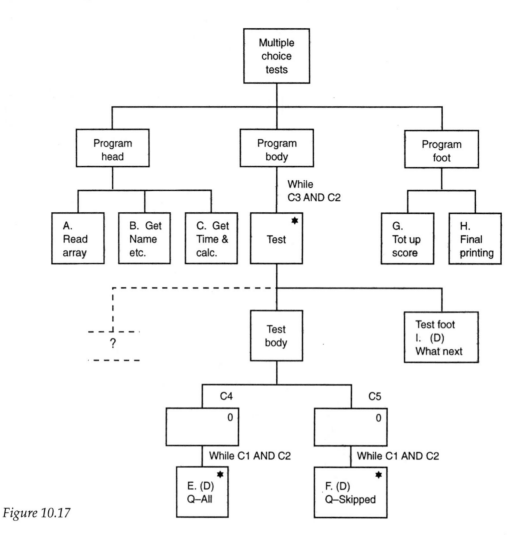

Figure 10.17

Figure 10.18

Initial screen (B)

Action list

7. write prompt for name
8. read i_name
9. write prompt for ref code
10. read i_ref_code
11. write i_array_no_qs[1]
12. write pass_mark[1]
13. write mins_allowed[1]
14. write prompt asking candidate to press Enter to begin and read for press of return

Condition list.

There are no conditions
See Fig. 10.19.

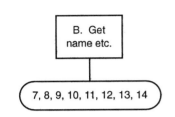

Figure 10.19

Get time and calculate end time (C)

Action list

15. (Get the time from the operating system. The actions will be system/language dependent.)
16. (Get the date from the operating system as above)
17. let w_secs_left = mins_allowed[1]*60
18. let w_end_secs = i_hr*60*60 + i_min*60 + i_sec + w_secs_left

Condition list

There are no conditions.
      See Fig. 10.20.

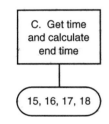

Figure 10.20

Q-All (E)

This is a more complex activity than the ones just dealt with, and it may be worth breaking it down into procedures, instead of going straight to an action list. There are three components: displaying the next question on the screen, getting a response from the candidate, and finding out how much time there is left. Because *W_secs_left* is compared with zero to decide whether to do another repeat (C2), the time remaining must be calculated after the candidate has made a response. If it were done the other way round, there might be quite a delay before the fact that time had run out was acted upon. A suitable diagram for Q-All would therefore be as shown in Fig. 10.21.

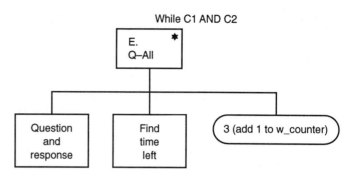

Figure 10.21

Question and response

Action list

19. write question[w_counter]
20. write choice_a[w_counter]
21. write choice_b[w_counter]
22. write choice_c[w_counter]
23. write choice_d[w_counter]
24. write prompt (for response to the question)
25. read o_resp[w_counter] (the response goes into an array)

Condition list

There are no conditions.

The diagram is just the sequence of actions 19–25, and can be appended to Fig. 10.21.

Find time left

Action list

26. (Get time from system. System/language dependent)
27. let w_time_secs_now = i_hr*60*60 + i_min*60 + i_sec
28. let w_secs_left = w_end_secs - w_time_secs_now

Again, there are no conditions and the three actions 26–28 can just be appended to the diagram above.

Q-skipped (F)

This is just the same as Q-All except that *W_counter* is handled differently. Initially, *W_counter* must be set to the number of the first skipped question, and when that one has been dealt with by the candidate, set to the number of the next skipped question. When there are no skipped questions left, *W_counter* should be one greater than *No_qs*[1], the number of questions in the test. Obviously, a procedure is needed to find the first, or next, skipped question - i.e. the next element of the array named *O_resp*, to contain 's'. Before dealing with that, a check needs to be made that W_counter has been initialized to 1, not only for Q-Skipped but for Q-All as well. Looking back, it appears that this has been overlooked. It needs to be before either part of Test body is entered, and therefore needs to be where Test head was before that was dropped. So action 2 needs using again, there.

Find next skipped

All that is needed here is to add 1 to *W_counter* (already listed as action 3) while ((the response in not 's') and (there are more questions)): i.e.

C5 while (w_counter <= no_qs[w_counter])
     AND (o_resp[w_counter] <> 's')

The diagram is as shown in Fig. 10.22. Q-Skipped can now be seen to be as in Fig. 10.23.

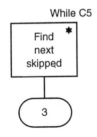

Figure 10.22

Test foot (or what next) (I)

This procedure provides the candidate with a little menu, and gets a choice: r, s or x. The creation of the menu consists of just writes of literals followed by the writing of a prompt. But the response must be checked, and the prompting be repeated if necessary until one of the three letters r, s or x is provided. *W_end_choice* needs initializing to a letter which is none of these, to make this possible. A repetition with test after would be suitable.

Action list

29. write menu literals
30. write prompt
31. read w_end_choice
32. let w_end_choice = 'a'

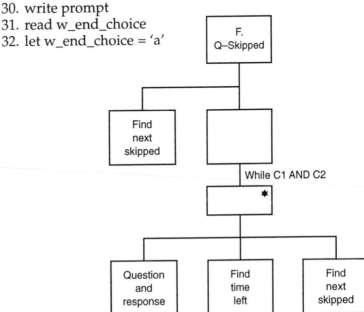

Figure 10.23

Condition

C6 w_end_choice = 'r' OR 's' OR 'x'

See Fig. 10.24.

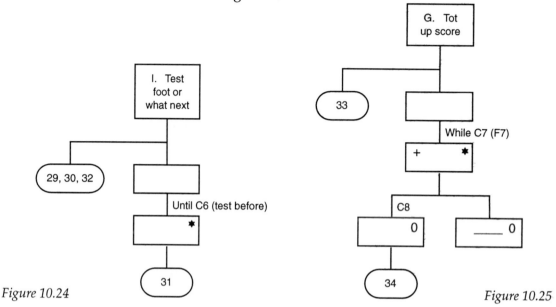

Figure 10.24

Figure 10.25

Tot up score (G)

There must be a run through the two arrays, and repeated comparison of the response with the answer. On a match, 1 must be added to *W_score*. A For will be good for this repetition, and because Pascal will have to have a local variable to control this, a new one, *Tsub*, is used.

Action list

33. let w_score = 0
34. add 1 to w_score

Condition and For list

C7 while tsub <= no_qs[1]
    F7 tsub from 1 by 1
C8 if ans[tsub] = o_resp[tsub]

See Fig. 10.25.

Final printing (H)

The print file is not yet ready for use and must be assigned and opened. The following then need doing:
● The score, together with other data from the first record of the input file needs printing.
● The verdict needs to be determined and printed.

- The two arrays need cycling through again, just as in Tot_up_score above, to print the numbers of the questions to which the right answer was not given.
- The array of responses needs cycling through again to print all the candidate's responses.
- A variable to control the FOR repetitions will again be needed and this will again be called Tsub.

Action list

35. assign print file
36. open print file
37. write test_ref[1] to print file
38. write w_date to print file
39. write i_name to print file
40. write w_score to print file
41. write pass_mark to print file
42. let w_verdict = 'Fail'
43. let w_verdict = 'Pass'
44. write w_verdict to print file
45. write tsub to print file
46. write tsub and o_resp to print file

Condition list

C7/F7   as above
C9 if w_score < pass_mark
C10 if o_resp <> ans[tsub]

See Fig. 10.26.

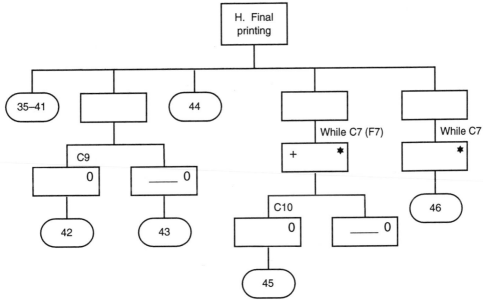

Figure 10.26

If no mistakes have been made (an unlikely event!) the design is now complete. It needs dry-running, touching up in the light of the errors found, and then coding.

If the design is checked carefully, or is coded and tested, it will be found to contain at least two errors:

- responses other than a, b, c, d, and s are allowed in answering questions;
- if time runs out whilst the candidate is in the screen that prompts for r, s or x, and r or s is chosen, the program presents a question and allows it to be answered.

A good design allows corrections to made with understanding and confidence. The correcting of these faults will now be discussed. The first concerns the procedure Question_and_response. Action 25 should be in a repetition: a repeat with test after would be fine.

Condition

C17 o_resp[w_counter] = 'a' OR 'b' OR 'c' OR 'd' OR 's'

See Fig. 10.27.

The second error, in What_next, arises because the time is not obtained and checked after a response is obtained, as it is in Q-All and Q-Skipped. The diagram should be as in Fig. 10.28.

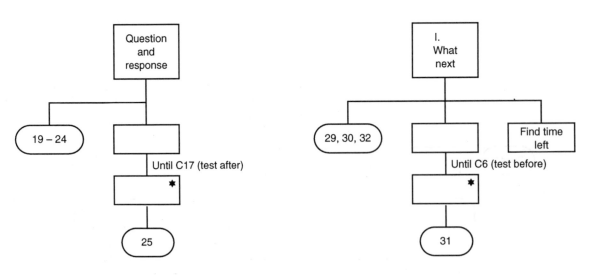

Figure 10.27   Figure 10.28

Exercises 10

10.1* The examining board is pleased with the program for multiple choice tests (above), but would like the following enhancements:

(a) as soon as the candidate has begun, by pressing Enter, the finishing time should be displayed on the screen.

(b) the What_next screen should show the candidate how much time, in whole minutes, is left, to help him/her in making a choice.

(c) if the candidate chooses to go through the skipped questions, and there are none, a message should be displayed, saying so.

Modify the design to incorporate them.

10.2 This question involves file handling with control breaks. It also involves the use of arrays, for decoding and for sorting. The decoding of colour, and the sorting of the six cars with the highest mileage, should be designed as subprograms.

Corncrake is a medium sized company dealing in used cars. The company normally has about 500 cars in stock, in all the branches combined. It keeps a computer file of all these vehicles. It is a serial file in sequence by *model* within *make* (that is, *make* is the major or primary key and *model* is the the minor or secondary one). The structure of the records on the file is given below.

Field	Type	Length
Make	X	12
Model	X	12
Engine size	NI	4 ml
Colour	X	2 a code; Letter + space or two letters
Year	NI	2
Doors	NI	1
Regn. No.	X	7
Mileage	NI	5
Location	NI	1 a code in the range 1 to 8

The output required is a list of all the cars. The lines should be single spaced, but a blank line is to be left between models. Every time *Make* changes there is to be a total showing the number of cars of that make, and each make is to start on a new page. Every page is to have headings and these should include a page number. At the end there should be a total showing how many cars there are altogether and in addition, a list of the six cars with the highest recorded mileage. Full particulars are to be given of each car, with colour and location decoded. The codes are shown in the Table.

Colour code	Full name	Location code	Full name
BK	Black	1	Peterborough
BU	Blue	2	Spalding
BN	Brown	3	Wisbech
G	Green	4	Market Deeping
R	Red	5	Boston
W	White		
Y	Yellow		

Note: The six cars with the highest mileage will be listed twice, once in the main report and again in the special list at the end.

10.3* Following the main examples in the chapter, draw up a design for the operation of a cash dispensing machine. The way it operates is as follows.

The automatic teller
The problem will be to design a program to simulate the actions of a bank cash dispensing machine. The one described here is an uncommon one, but it is real one in daily use at the time of writing. Briefly, you insert a plastic card which has a magnetic stripe on, key in your personal identification number (PIN), key in the amount of money you want, and out it pops. There are no paying-in facilities. There is a keypad with 16 keys, as in the diagram. The central block of keys is white. The three keys on the left are blue. The Cancel key is red, and the Proceed key is green. There is a small screen. A receipt may be printed. Details of every transaction are printed anyway on a till roll available to the bank but not the customer.

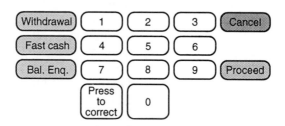

The machine is, therefore, a terminal to a large computer. We will assume this to be a mainframe at the bank's head office. The terminal consists of two input devices: the keyboard and the magnetic stripe reader; and four output devices: the screen, the bank-note dispenser, the printer that prints the till roll and the printer that prints the receipts. The customer master file, a direct access file, is permanently online, and provides an additional source of data.

Adaptations and simplifications

- For our simulation, we shall assume a microcomputer is being used.

- The key A will be substituted for putting the card in the slot.
- The keying of an account number will be substituted for the reading of a stripe.
- For the Withdraw key: the 'W' key;
- For the Fast Cash key: the 'F' key;
- for the Balance Enquiry key: the 'B' key;
- For the Press to Correct key: the 'C' key;
- for the Proceed key: the 'P' key;
- For the Cancel key: the 'X' key.
- For the two different printers: two print files,
- The machine that dispenses the bank notes will be ignored. The fact that the money was dispensed, as recorded on the till roll, will be sufficient.
- The removal of the card from its slot will be replaced by keying E (for end of transaction).
- The whole customer file will be read into an array in main store at the start of the program, and updated there. At the end of the program it will be written back. (This could not be done in practice; the file would be far too big to fit into the main store of even a large computer.)

In reality, if a customer does not respond to any prompt within 10 seconds, the transaction is terminated. It is difficult to simulate this in Pascal, Cobol or Basic, so you should ignore this requirement.

The sequence of events

This relates to use by one customer.

1. 'A' is keyed (card going in slot). Program gets date and time from system.

2. Account number is keyed (stripe read). If the attempt to get a six digit number fails, the transaction is terminated.

3. Message displayed: 'Please enter your PIN'.

4. PIN is keyed. Prompting is repeated until a four digit number bigger than 0 is entered.

5. Message displayed: 'Choose transaction, W, F or B'.

6. One of those letters is keyed. Three tries are allowed. If the third is not one of these letters, the transaction is terminated.

7. Message displayed: 'Your request is being processed'.

8. The records in the array are scanned in an attempt to locate the customer's record. If it is not found, the message 'Faulty card. Transaction terminated. Please remove your card.' is displayed and removal simulated by the 'E' key. If it is found, the PIN is checked. If this does not agree with what was keyed, a message is displayed: 'Incorrect PIN – Please try again'. The customer is allowed three tries. If

the PIN is still not the one on file, there is display of the message 'Incorrect PIN – transaction terminated – Please remove your card', and the transaction is terminated. A note of this failure is made on the audit roll: the customer number, the time and the last incorrect PIN keyed.

9. If 'B' is keyed (Balance Enquiry), the current balance, taken from the customer record in the array, is displayed on the screen. After 10 seconds, the screen clears and the card is offered for removal, together with the message 'Please remove your card'.

10. If 'W' is keyed (General withdrawal), the message displayed is: 'If you want a receipt key 1, else key 0'. The prompt is held until one or the other of those keys is pressed.

11. Message displayed: 'Key in amount in pounds, as a multiple of 10'.

12. If the amount keyed is not a multiple of 10 or is over 200, a message is displayed pointing out the error, held for about 10 seconds, and then the 'Key in amount...' message is repeated.

13. Message displayed: '£nn entered. Press 'Proceed' if correct, or 'Press to correct' if not.

14. If 'press to correct' is chosen, it returns to step 11.

15. If 'Proceed' is chosen, the customer record in the array in store is updated. If it would become less than zero, the transaction is terminated, with the message: 'Insufficient funds'. Otherwise the message is 'New balance is £nnnn'.

16. Card is pushed out. Message becomes 'Please remove your card'.

17. If a receipt was requested it is printed and presented.

18. Transaction is logged by printing on the audit roll the figures: account number, amount, new balance, time.

19. The money is counted and presented.

20. If 'F' (Fast Cash) was entered, steps 10 to 14 are skipped, and the amount of money wanted is assumed to be £30.

Assumptions

(i)   Assume there are instructions or functions that obtain the time and date from the operating system.

(ii) Assume the program can be terminated by a clerk pressing a key which customers cannot reach. He/she uses this only when no customer is using the machine. Use the Q key for this in your design.

(iii) Assume there are no other keys than 0–9 and W,F,B,C,P,X,E and Q. All other keys should be ignored by the program, or treated as errors.

Answers to Exercises

Chapter 2

2.1 c, g and h are not conditions. c is an instruction or an invitation, but it cannot be said to be true or false. In g there is no operator. The expression simply evaluates to 8. In h, >< is not an operator. It has no meaning.

2.2 See Fig. A1.

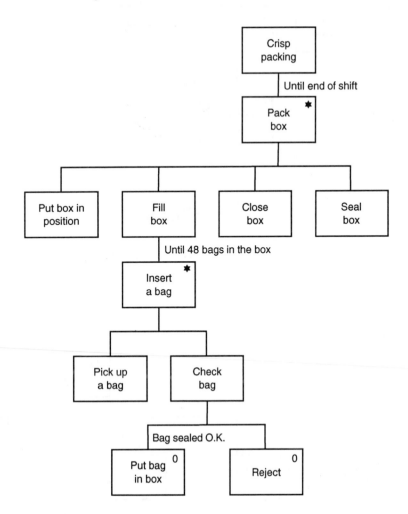

Figure A1

2.3   See Fig. A2.

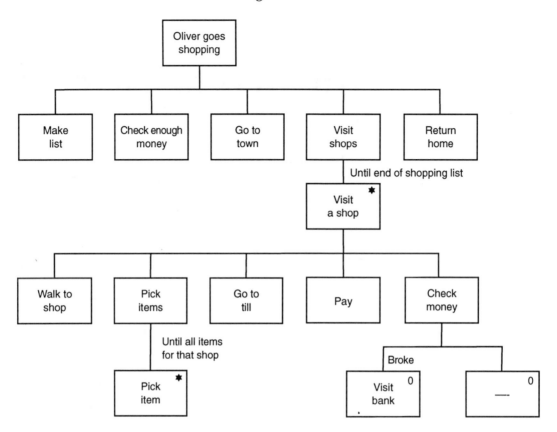

Figure A2

Chapter 3

3.1   See Fig. A3

3.2   The −1 would be added in, so the answer would be too small.

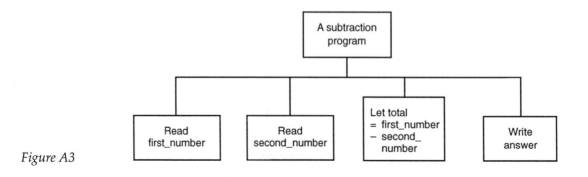

Figure A3

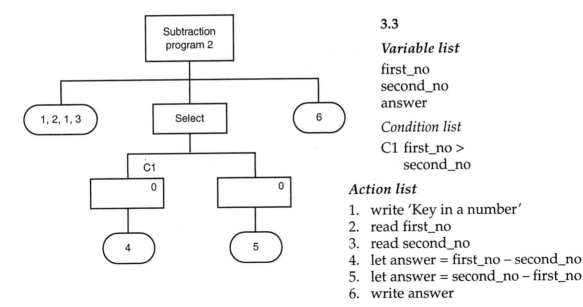

Figure A4

3.3

Variable list

first_no
second_no
answer

Condition list

C1 first_no >
   second_no

Action list

1. write 'Key in a number'
2. read first_no
3. read second_no
4. let answer = first_no – second_no
5. let answer = second_no – first_no
6. write answer

See Fig. A4

3.4

Variable list

first_no
second_no
choice

Condition list
C1 Choice = 'A'

Action list

1. write 'Key in a number'
2. read first_no
3. read second_no
4. let answer = first_no – second_no
5. let answer = first_no + second_no
6. write answer
7. write 'Type A for add or S for subtract'
8. read choice

See Fig. A5

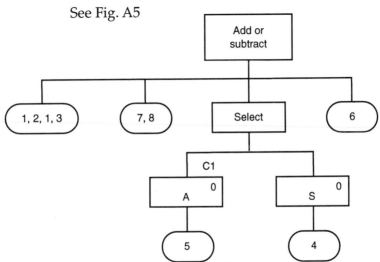

Figure A5

3.6

Variable list	*Action list*
number_1	1. write number_1
number_2	2. write number_2
number_3	3. write number_3
	4. read number_1
Condition list	5. read number_2
C1 number_1 > number_2	6. read number_3
C2 number_1 > number_3	7. write 'Key a number'
C3 number_2 > number_3	

See Fig. A6

Note: There are many other solutions to this problem.

3.7 You need to check with three different combinations such as 10, 12, 12; 10, 10, 12; and 12, 10, 12. The solution given above would work without alteration. If, for number 6, you had based your solution on the one in the chapter that uses six compound conditions, your solution would not have worked. It could have been made to work by changing all the '>' signs in the conditions to '>='.

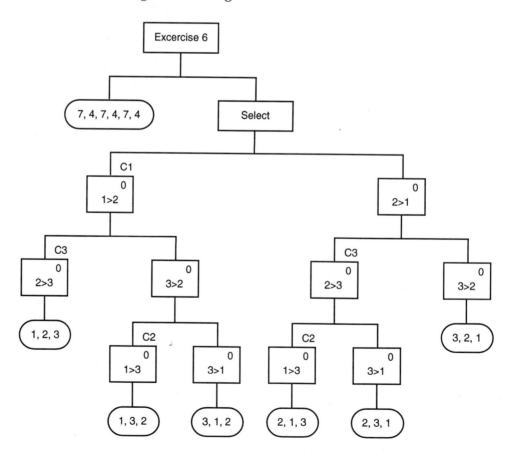

Figure A6

Chapter 4

4.1

Variable list	*Action list*

Variable list

word_1
word_2
word_3
again

Condition list

C1   word_1 < word_2
C2   word_1 < word_3
C3   word_2 < Word_3'
C4   again = 'N'

Action list

1. write word_1
2. write word_2
3. write word_3
4. read word_1
5. read word_2
6. read word_3
7. write 'Key a word'
8. write 'Another set (Y/N)?'
9. read again

See Fig. A7
1. The lettering of the boxes is for the solution to 4.3.
2. There are many other solutions to this problem.

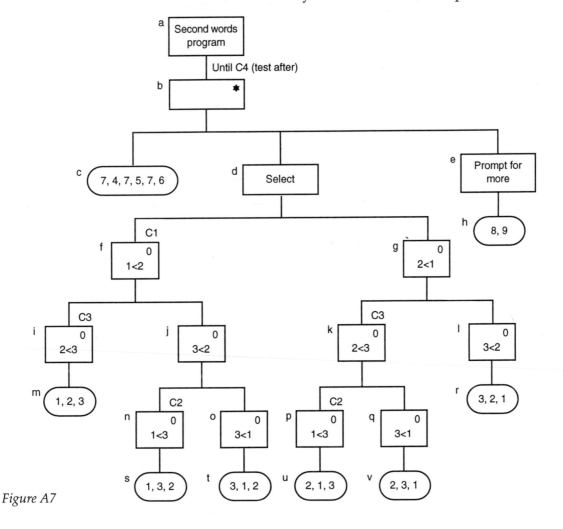

Figure A7

4.2

Variable list	*Action list*
first_no	1. write 'Key in a number'
second_no	2. read first_no
answer	3. read second_no
again	4. let answer = first_no − second_no
	5. let answer = second_no − first_no
Condition list	6. write answer
C1 first_no >	7. write 'Another (Y/N)? '
second_no	8. read again
C2 again <> 'Y'	

See Fig. A8

Note: The lettering of the boxes is for the solution to 4.4.

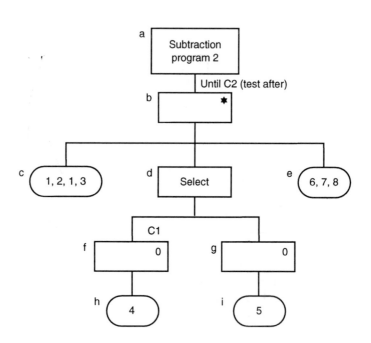

Figure A8

4.3 (i)

Step	word_1	word_2	word_3	again	C1	C2	C3	C4	Outcome
a	?	?	?	?	?	?	?	?	
b									
c	up	the	pole						
d					False				
g							False		
l									
r									pole the
e									up
h				Y					
b								False	
c	history	is	bunk						
d					True				
f							False		
j						False			
o									
t									bunk history
e									is
h				N					
b								True	
a									

4.3 (ii)

Step	first_no	second_no	answer	again	C1	C2			Outcome
a	?	?	?	?	?	?	?	?	
b									
c	15	15							
d					False				
g									
i			0						
e				Y					0
b						False			
c	8	12							
d					True				
f									
h			4						
e				Y					4
b						False			
c	4856	2754							
d					False				
g									
i			2102						
e				N					2102
b						True			
a									

4.4   Apart from changing the word 'Until' to 'While' on the diagram, the Conditions need changing to:

C1 again = 'Y'
C2 counter < list-length

Note that if C2 is made

C2 counter <= list-length,

then action 3 needs changing to

3.   let counter = 1,

or the repetition will be done too many times

Chapter 5

5.1   There will be a main repetition, presenting the opening menu. There will be a subroutine associated with each choice (except Quit). There will be a repetition in each subroutine, to display the message again if R is pressed. Because the program does not do anything useful, very few variables are needed. One will be needed to control the main repetition. That is called Choice in the list below. Another will be needed to control the repetitions in the subprograms. That is called Decision. A third is needed for the 'Press Enter' when an error is made. That is called Dummy.

Variables		*Condition list*
choice	C	C1 choice = '1'
decision	C	C2 choice = '2'
dummy	C	C3 choice = '3'
		C4 choice = '4'
		C5 choice = '5'

Action list

1.   Write the menu (note that this is several statements)
2.   Write the prompt
3.   Read choice
4.   Write 'That was not a valid choice'
5.   Read dummy

For the diagram, see Fig. A9

   Although action 5, read dummy, gets a character into the variable called dummy, it does not matter what this is. The purpose of action 5 is just to get the Enter key pressed.
   Refinement of any of List, Modify, Delete, Add:

Action list

6.   write appropriate message
7.   display prompt 'R' or 'Q'
8.   read decision

For the diagram, see Fig. A10

Figure A9

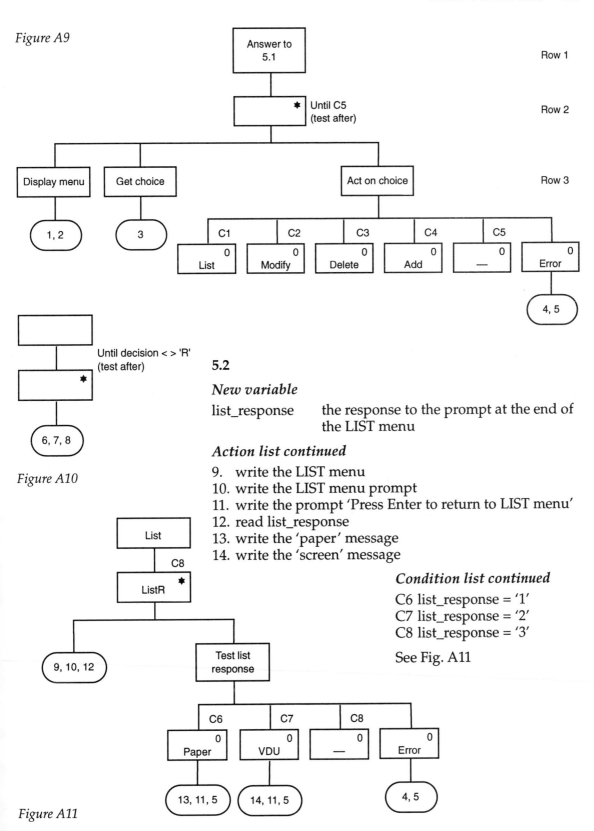

Row 1

Row 2

Row 3

Figure A10

5.2

New variable

list_response   the response to the prompt at the end of the LIST menu

Action list continued

9. write the LIST menu
10. write the LIST menu prompt
11. write the prompt 'Press Enter to return to LIST menu'
12. read list_response
13. write the 'paper' message
14. write the 'screen' message

Condition list continued

C6 list_response = '1'
C7 list_response = '2'
C8 list_response = '3'

See Fig. A11

Figure A11

5.3

New variable

vdu_response   the response to the prompt at the end of the VDU MENU

Action list continued

15. write the VDU menu
16. write the VDU menu prompt
17. read vdu_response
18. write the 'first twenty' message
19. write the 'last twenty' message
20. write the 'whole file' message
21. write the 'one-in-ten' message
22. read press_enter
23. write 'Press enter to continue '

Condition list continued

C9   vdu_response = '1'
C10   vdu_response = '2'
C11   vdu_response = '3'
C12   vdu_response = '4'
C13   vdu_response = '5'

See Fig. A12

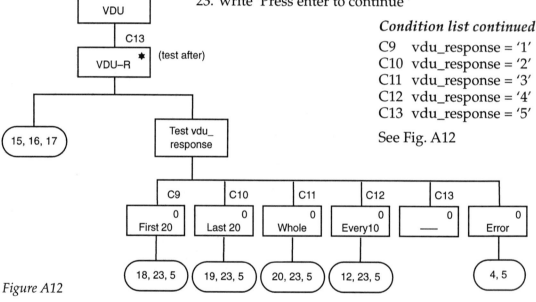

Figure A12

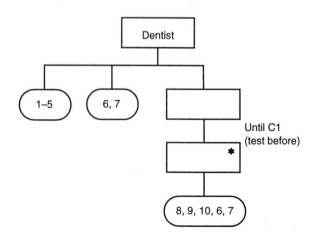

Figure A13

Chapter 6

6.1

Variable list

price		a 5-element array of NI
name		string
work_type	NI	
no_teeth	NI,	number of teeth for this patient
charge	NI	

Action list

1. let price[1] = 14
2. let price[2] = 10
3. let price[3] = 50
4. let price[4] = 25
5. let price[5] = 20
6. write prompt
7. read name
8. read work_type, no_teeth
9. let charge = price[work_type] * no_teeth
10. write name, charge

Condition list

C1 name = 'XXXX'

For the diagram, see Fig. A13 on page 150.

6.2

Variable list

nmbr	NI	a number input
mean	ND	the mean or average
array		a 200-element array of NI
difference	ND	the difference between the mean and a number
j	NI	a subscript and counter
total	NI	the total of all numbers read
length	NI	the number of numbers input – that is, the active length of the array.

Action list

1. let array[j] = nmbr
2. let j = 1
3. add 1 to j
4. let difference = array[j] - mean
5. add nmbr to total
6. let mean = total / length
7. read nmbr
8. let total = 0

9. let length = j - 1
10. write a prompt
11. write 'Mean is ', mean
12. write array[j], difference

Condition list

C1 nmbr = -999
C2 j > 200
C3 j > length

See Fig. A14

Figure A14

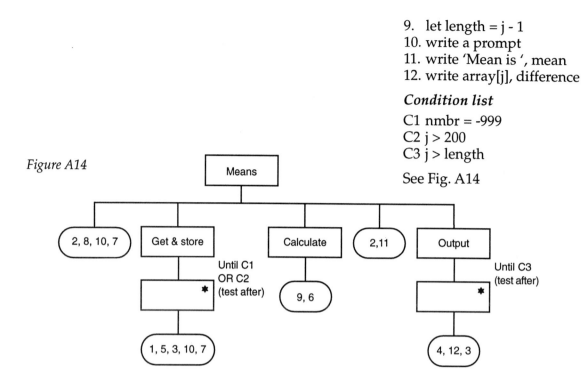

6.3

Variable list

month_nmbr	NI
name_array	a 12-element array of strings
month_name	

Action list

1.   let name_array[1] = 'January'
2.   let name_array[2] = 'February'
4–12 similar
13. let month_name = name_array[month_nmbr]

There are no conditions.

The diagram is just a sequence, although in a real program, actions 1–12 would be right at the beginning and action 13 would be elsewhere and repeated

See Fig. A15

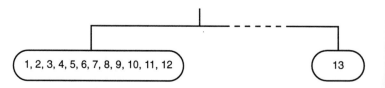

Figure A15

6.4 It will be assumed that day_abbrev always contains one of the seven pairs of letters in the question and never anything else.

Variable list

day_abbrev	X	
name_array	a 12-element array of X	
abbrev_array	a 12-element array of X	
day_name	X	
j	NI	a counter and subscript

Action list

1.   let name_array[1] = 'Monday'
2.   let name_array[2] = 'Tuesday'
4–7   similar
8.   let abbrev_array[1] = 'Mo'
9.   let abbrev_array[2] = 'Tu'
10–14 similar
15.   let day_name = name_array[j]
16.   let j = 0
17.   add 1 to j

Condition list

C1 day_abbrev = abbrev_array[j]

See Fig. A16

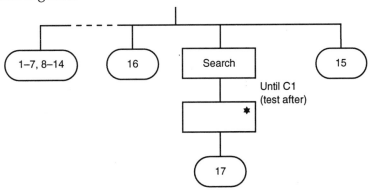

Figure A16

6.6 Start by looking carefully at the example, the working for 583614.

$$4 \times 2 + 1 \times 1 + 6 \times 2 + 3 \times 1 + 8 \times 2 + 5 \times 1$$
$$= 8 + 1 + 12 + 3 + 16 + 5 = 45$$

45/17 = 2 remainder 11.
17 − 11 = 06.
The number becomes 58361406.
(If the remainder is 0, append 17 − 0 = 17;
if the remainder is 16, append 17 − 16 = 01.)

The given number needs putting into an array so that its digits can be dealt with individually (or in pairs). How this would be done would depend on the language used. The first calculation step is to do the multiplying and adding. The digits can be dealt with in pairs, and they can be accumulated into a total variable (called Step1 below) as they are multiplied by their weightings. The second step is to divide by 17 and find the remainder (giving Step2). The third step is to subtract the remainder from 17 (giving Step3). Finally Step3 needs 'sticking on the end of' the original number. This means getting the number out of the array, so making it one whole number again, multiplying it by 100 and adding Step3. It is extracted from the array here in the second repetition. Using the example number above, 583614, the successive values of New would be:

0;   0, 5;   50, 8;   580, 583   5830, 5836;
58360, 58361;   583610, 583614

Variable list		*Condition list*
Num_array (a 6-element array of NI)		C1 $j = 0$
j	NI	C2 $j > 6$
step1	NI	
step2	ND	
step3	ND	
new	NI	

Action list

1. let Step1 = 0
2. let Step1 = step1 + (Num_array[j] * 2) + (num_array[j-1])
3. let Step2 = remainder from step1 / 17

Note. C, Pascal and Cobol all have ways of obtaining a remainder easily, but they are all different.

4. let step3 = 17 – step2
5. let j = 6
6. let j = j - 2
7. let j = 1
8. add 1 to j
9. let new = 0
10. let new = new * 10
11. let new = new + num_array[j]
12. let new = new * 100
13. let new = new + step3

Now the diagram can be drawn (Fig. A17).

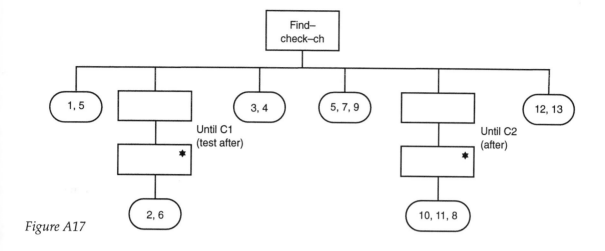

Figure A17

6.7 The only change that needs to be made is to use >
instead of < in condition C3:

C3 wword[j+1] < wword[j] must be changed to
C3 wword[j+1] > wword[j].

Chapter 7

7.1 This solution assumes that the system detects end of
file when an attempt to read a record fails.

Sample data				Results expected				
O	56	2		O	56	2	112	112
S	20	1		S	20	1	20	18
S	30	3		S	30	3	90	88
O	40	4		O	40	4	160	144
S	50	5		S	50	5	250	223

Two customers received the 10% discount

Variable list

Input
spring-rec	the name of the input record
s-cust-type	C 'S' or 'O'
s-quant	N
s-item-price	N

Output
gross-cost	N
amount-due	N
ten-pc-tot	N

Action list

1. open spring file
2. close spring file
3. read a record, spring-rec, from spring file
4. let gross-cost = s-quant * s-item-price
5. let amount-due = gross-cost * 0.9
6. add 1 to ten-pc-tot
7. let amount-due = gross-cost
8. let amount-due = amount-due - 2
9. let ten-pc-tot = 0
10. write s-cust-type, s-quant, s-item-price, gross-cost, amount-due
11. write ten-pc-tot, ' customers received the 10% discount.'

Condition list

C1 end of spring file
C2 gross-cost > 150
C3 s-cust-type = 'S'

For the diagram, see Fig. A18

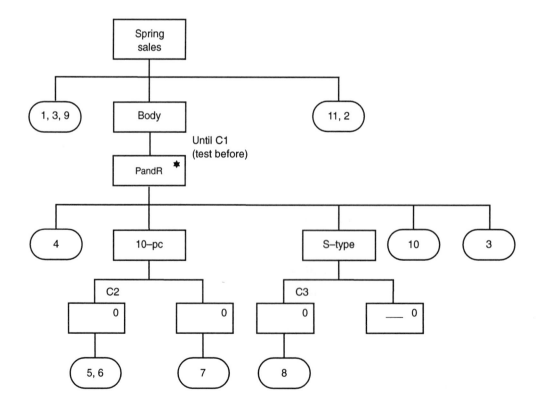

Figure A18

7.3 It will be assumed that records for non-existent branches are on the file, with the word 'error' in place of the branch name, and also that end of file is detected by the program function EOF when the last record is read.

Variables

Input	*Output*
k-branch-num	o-branch-name
(keyboard)	
f-branch-name	

(the one-field record on the file called Branch-file)

Working
branch-name   (a 10 element array)
sub   (a subscript and counter)

Action list
1. write branch-name[k-branch-num]
2. open Branch file
3. close Branch file
4. read f-branch-num
5. let branch-name[sub] = f-branch-name
6. let sub = 1
7. add 1 to sub
8. write prompt for branch number
9. let k-branch-num = 0
10. read k-branch-num (from keyboard)

Condition list

C1 eof is true
C2 k-branch-num = 99
See Fig. A19

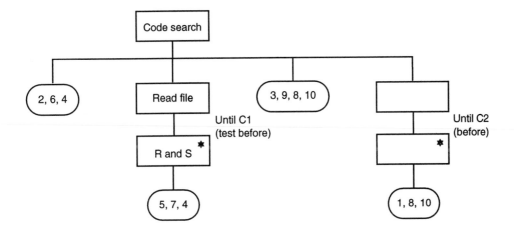

Figure A19

7.5   After the dates have been obtained and before the main processing is entered, records must be read from the file until the first date is found. Subsequently, the date on each record must be inspected and processing terminated as soon as the second date is found.

New input variables *(from keyboard)*	*New conditions*
first-d-date	C4 deliv-date > last-d-date
last-d-date	C5 deliv-date >= first-d-date

New actions
16. write prompt for first-d-date
17. read first-d-date from keyboard
18. write prompt for last-d-date
19. read prompt for last-d-date

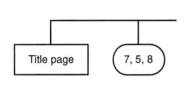

Figure A20

The diagram in Fig. A20 becomes like that in Fig. A21

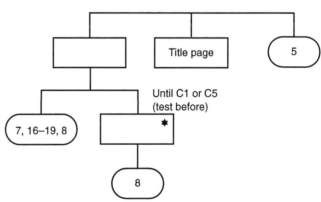

Figure A21

Where there was C1 on its own before there will need to be C1 OR C4

Where there was C1 OR C2 before, C1 OR C2 OR C4 will be needed. And where there was C1 OR C2 OR C3 before, C1 OR C2 OR C3 OR C4 will be needed.

7.4

Variables

applicant file record:	fields in output lines:
name	code-count
course	code-average-points
code	course-count
points	course-average-points
field in heading:	work fields:
heading-course	code-total
	course-total
	stored-code
	stored-course

Action list

1. open applicant-file
2. read record from applicant-file
3. let code-total = 0
4. let course-total = 0
5. let code-count = 0
6. let course-count = 0
7. write code-average-points
8. write code-count
9. close applicant-file
10. write course-average-points
11. write course-count
12. let heading-course = stored-course
13. write page heading after form-feed
14. let stored-course = course
15. let stored-code = code
16. add 1 to code-total
17. add 1 to course-total
18. write to printer all input fields
19. compute code-average-points
    = code-total/code-count
20. compute course-average-points
    = course-total / course-count
21. add points to course-total
22. add points to code-total

Condition list

C1 end of applicant file
C2 end of applicant file OR stored-course NOT
   = course
C3 end of applicant file OR stored-course NOT
   = course
   OR stored-code NOT = code

See Fig. A22

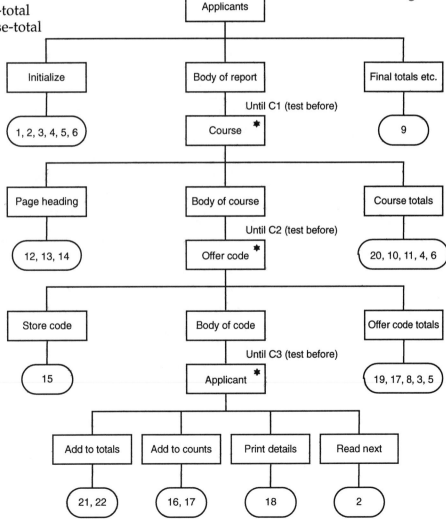

Figure A22

Chapter 8

8.1 In outline, the design will be as in Fig. A23, unless an error message is required.

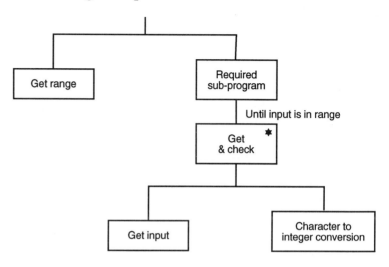

Figure A23

The main procedure, Character to integer conversion, is unchanged. For the rest, a few more actions and conditions will be necessary.

Extra actions

10. write prompt for bottom of range, min
11. read min
12. write prompt for top of range, max
13. read max
14. write prompt for s-prompt (that is, ask for what words the new subroutine should use)
15. read s-prompt
16. write the prompt s-prompt
17. read number (into the array of characters called in-arr)

Extra condition

C4 o-number >= min AND o-number <= max

See Fig. A24

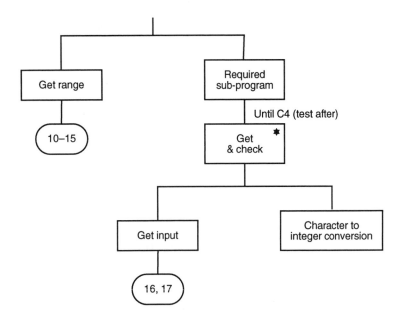

Figure A24

8.2   Most of the changes will be within the part at present labelled 'Language specific'. It must be be assumed that at an early stage the input will be in the array of characters called in_array. Before anything else is done, any sign must be moved to a separate variable, which might be called Sign. If there is no sign the number will be assumed to be positive.

Extra actions	*Extra conditions*
15. let sign = '+'	C7 in-arr[1] = '+'
16. let sign = '-'	C8 in-arr[1] = '-'
17. let in-arr[1] = '0'	C9 sign = '-'
18. let o-number = o-number ∗ – 1	

In the language specific part, at the beginning, as soon as the keyed input is in *In-arr*, the diagram will be as in Fig. A25.

Right at the end, after 'Position point' as in Fig. A26.

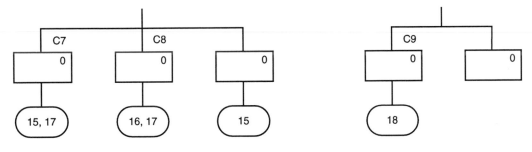

Figure A25   *Figure A26*

8.3   This problem follows the same general form as the shoe shop example in the chapter. An outline high level design is not difficult and could be as follows:

Action list

1. write prompt 'are you sure '
2. read confirm from keyboard
3. let station = '   '
4. let confirm = ' '   *Condition list*
10. open output disk file   C1 station = 'XXXX'
11. close disk file   C2 confirm = 'Y'

For the diagram, see Fig. A27
In 'Get station', the station name is prompted for, and a name is accepted, until four non-blank characters are received from

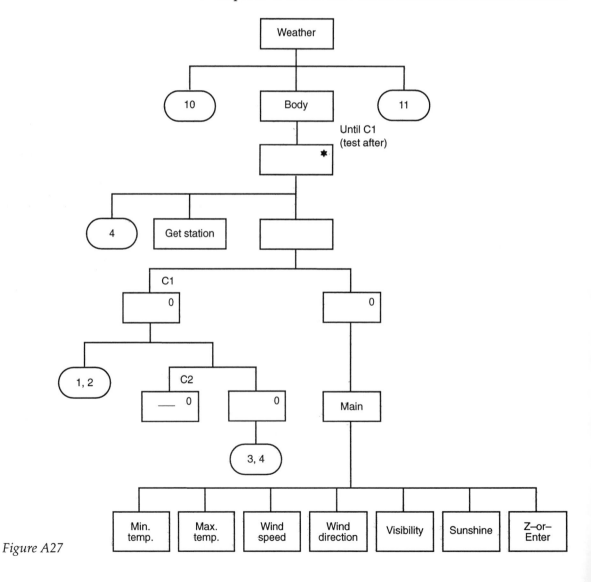

Figure A27

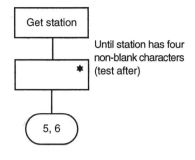

Figure A28

Until station has four
non-blank characters
(test after)

the keyboard. The way this is tested for will be language specific, so the condition is shown below informally.

Actions

5. write prompt for station name
6. read station from keyboard

See Fig. A28

In 'Min temp', preparations are made for calling 'Get signed int', and it is then called. 'Get signed int' is a sub-program developed from the answers to 8.1 and 8.2, that is, a sub-program that accepts a maximum, a minimum and a prompt (8.1), and allows a sign (8.2). As this weather problem features maximum and minimum temperatures, the parameters for passing 'Get signed int' will be re-named *Low* and *High*.

Actions

7. let low = -20
8. let high = 35
9. let prompt = 'Key min temp '

For the diagram, see Fig. A29

Max temp, Wind speed, Wind direction and Sunshine are all similar, except that Sunshine calls 'Get decimal number', which can be adapted from the design in the chapter called 'Character to number with decimal point'. This can be done by the same means as were used in your answer to 8.1 to adapt 'Character to integer conversion'. The actions needed will be

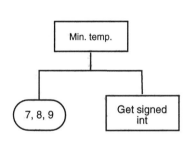

Figure A29

Actions

In Max temp:
12. let low = min (the value returned by 'Get signed int')

In Min temp:
13. let high = 45
14. let prompt = 'Key max temp'
In Wind speed:
15. let low = 0
16. let high = 130
17. let prompt = 'Key wind speed'
In Wind direction:
18. let low = 0
19. let high = 259
20. let prompt = 'Key wind direction'
In Sunshine:
21. let low = 0.00
22. let high = 22.00
23. let prompt = 'Key hours of sunshine'

Visibility will be just like the getting of Payment-method in

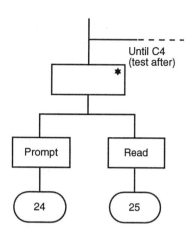

Figure A30

the shoe shop example:

Action list

24. write 'Key in visibility (B, P, F or G) '
25. read visibility

Condition list

C4 visibility = 'B' OR 'P' OR 'F' OR 'G'

See Fig. A30

The last box in the main sequence, Z-or-enter, determines whether anything is to be written to disk or not. Suppose 'Z', if keyed, goes into the field called *Verdict*.

New variable

verdict

Action list

26. let verdict = ' '
27. write 'Enter to confirm, Z to abandon '
28. read verdict
29. write four input fields to disk
30. write all keyed data to disk file
31. write 'record abandoned'
32. write 'record written to disk file'

Condition list

C5 verdict = 'Z'

For the diagram, see Fig. A31

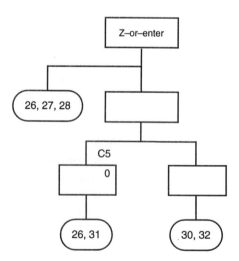

Figure A31

Chapter 9

9.1

```
SUBPROGRAM t
 REPEAT
    WRITE prompt for height
    READ height
 UNTIL height is numeric
 REPEAT
    WRITE prompt for weight
    READ weight
 UNTIL weight is numeric
 LET factor = weight / height
 IF factor < 0.34 THEN
    WRITE 'thin'
 ELSE
    IF factor > o.49 THEN
        WRITE 'fat'
    ELSE
        WRITE 'No problem'
    ENDIF
 ENDIF
 WRITE 'Press enter to return to the menu'
 READ k
ENDSUBPROGRAM
```

9.2

```
SUBPROGRAM Find-check-ch
 LET step2 = 0
 LET flag =  '  '
 FOR J FROM 1 BY 1 UNTIL J > 4
    LET weighting = 4 + 2 - j
    LET step2 = step2 + num-array[j]
                * weighting
 ENDFOR
 LET step3 = remainder from
             dividing step2 by 11
 IF step3 = 0 THEN
    LET ch-did = 0
 ELSE
    IF step3 = 1 THEN
        LET flag = 'X'
    ELSE
        LET ch-dig = 11 - step3
    ENDIF
 ENDIF
ENDSUBPROGRAM
```

Chapter 10

10.2   Assumptions:
1. The six cars with the highest mileage will be listed twice, once in the main report and in the special list at the end.
2. All the data are valid, so that, for instance, colour code will always be one of the seven codes listed in the question.

Answer: The program is a control-break program, but it incorporates both decoding and sorting. The sort (for the cars with the highest mileage) will be copied from the one given in the chapter on arrays.

Variable list

From file
Record name is car-rec

Field	Type	Length	
Make	X	12	
Model	X	12	
Engine-size	NI	4	ml
Col-code	X	2	a code; Letter + space or two letters
Year	NI	2	
Doors	NI	1	
Regn. No.	X	7	
Mileage	NI	5	
Loc-code	NI	1	a code in the range 1 to 8

Output

All the input (except col-code and loc-code, which will be replaced by words)

colour	X	grand-total	NI
location	X	page-no	NI
make-total	NI		

Other variables

Five arrays are needed:

loc-array	an array of location names
col-array	an array of colours (words in full)
cc-array	an array of colour codes
mi-array	an array of the six highest mileages
rec-array	an array of the output records for the six cars with the highest mileages

also needed are:

j	a subscript
stored-make	so we can see when make changes
stored-model	so we can see when model changes
swaps	a boolean, for the sort
temp-mi	for mileage when swapping in the sort
temp-rec	for the full record when swapping in the sort

Action list

1. open car-file
2. read record from car-file
3. let mi-array[j] = 0
4. let grand-total = 0
5. let make-total = 0
6. let page-no = 0
7. write rec-array[j]
8. let j = 1
9. add 1 to j
10. write grand-total
11. close car-file
12. add 1 to page-no
13. write page heading after form-feed
14. let stored-make = make
15. write make-total
16. let stored-model = model
17. write blank line
18. add 1 to make-total
19. add 1 to model-total
20. let location = loc-array[loc-code]
21. let colour = col-array[j]
22. write write all input fields (except col-code and loc-code), and location and colour
23. let mi-array[6] = mileage
24. let col-array[1] = 'Black'
25. let col-array[2] = 'Blue '
26–30 similar for Brown, Green, Red, White, Yellow
31. let cc-array[1] = 'BK'
32. let cc-array[2] = 'BU'
33–37 similar for BN, G, R, W, Y
38. let loc-array[1] = 'Peterborough'
39. let loc-array[2] = 'Spalding'
40–42 similar for Wisbech, Market Deeping and Boston
43. let rec-array[6] = the output record just printed

Condition list

C1 end of car-file
C2 end of car-file OR make NOT = stored-make
C3 end of car-file OR make NOT = stored-make
   OR model NOT = stored-model
C4 mileage > mi-array[6]
C5 j > 6

See Figs. A32a and A32b

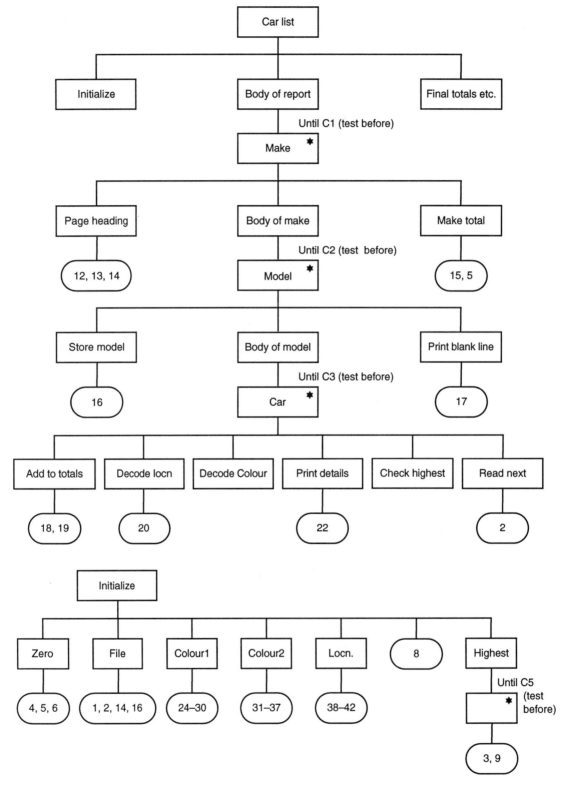

Figure A32a

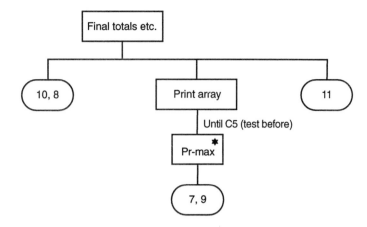

Figure A32b

To decode colour, two extra conditions will be needed:

Condition and For list

C6 j > 7
   F6 from 1 by 1
C7 col-code = cc-array[j]

See Fig.A33

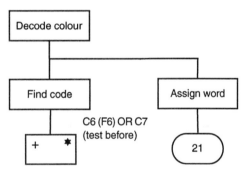

Figure A33

For the sub-program Check highest, the reasoning will be this. The mileage will be compared with the lowest of the six in the array called Highest-array (which will be in position 6). If it is higher, it will be assigned to position 6, overwriting what was there, and the contents of the array will be sorted, using the simple sort given in Chapter 6. If it is not higher, nothing will be done.

Action list

51. let swaps = false
52. let swaps = true
53. let temp-mi = mi-array[j+1]
54. let mi-array[j+1] = mi-array[j]
55. let mi-array[j] = temp-mi

56. let temp-rec = rec-array[j + 1]
57. let rec-array[j +1] = rec-array[j]
58. Let rec-array[j] = temp-rec

Condition and For list

C8   swaps = false
C9   (j+1) > 6
F9   j from 1 by 1
C10 mi-array[j+1] > mi-array[j]
C11 j > 6
F11 j from 1 by 1

The comparison used in C9 involves (j+1) not j because C10 involves (j+1). This is because each element in the array is compared with the one higher up, until there is no relevant data in the one higher up, or the end of the array is reached.
    See Fig. A34

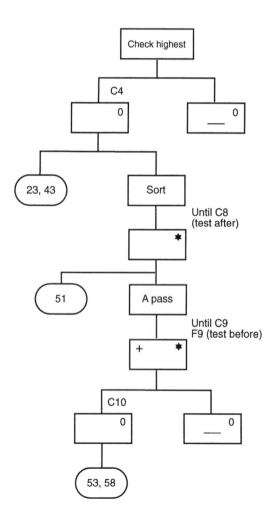

Figure A34

Index

All words in the index are printed in bold in the text the first time they are used. (Not all words in bold are in the index, though.)